Hypogeans
Space that Matters

Edited by Rubén Alcolea

faber
press

The work compiled in this volume was
produced as a result of the Graduate Studio
Arch515.01 Hypogeans, which took place
at Roger Williams University during the fall
semester 2021.

Faculty:
Rubén Alcolea

Students:
Mitchell Dasilva
Anakin Geisler
Brooke McDermott
Lauren Ostrzyzek
Jessica Raccio
Mark Reul
Robert Rice
Lisett Ronchi
Adam Royle
Lauren Scheid
Kyle Sheehan
Brianna Valcourt
Robert Ward

Final Reviews Critics:
Rubén Alcolea
Christopher Bardt
Julian Bonder
Ginette Castro
Ryan Ludwig
Steve White
Dinglinang Yang

Hypogeans. Space that Matters
114 p. / 8x10 in / 20.32x25.40 cm

ISBN 979-8-218-02459-8
2022

Publisher:
faber press
www.faberpress.com

Editor:
Rubén Alcolea

Layout:
Jessica Raccio

Cover image:
Interior by Brooke McDermott

Roger Williams
University

Cummings School of Architecture
Roger Williams University
One Old Ferry Road
Bristol, Rhode Island 02809, USA
www.rwu.edu

Hypogeans
Space that Matters

The difference between landscape and landscape is small, but there are great differences in the beholders. There is nothing so wonderful in any particular landscape, as the necessity of being beautiful under which every landscape lies. Nature cannot be surprised in undress. Beauty breaks in everywhere.

– Ralph Waldo Emerson, "Nature",
in Essays, Second series, 1844, 4.

Caspar Friedrich
Tombs of the Old Heroes, 1812
Kunsthalle, Hamburg

Introduction

The anthropological relationship between humans and nature defines a fundamental basis for the creation of architecture. The necessity to build in the wilderness resulted in a beautiful symbiosis which characterized the origin of architecture at the beginning of civilization. Although nature may be understood now as the antithesis of the built environment, any creation of space requires a clear understanding of the natural surroundings and the enhancement of the possibilities which arise from that fruitful conversation. The wild offers a place of mystery where darkness, shadows and sounds define the field to leave reason behind in favor of our senses. The narrative of western civilization since ancient times has generally called for the necessity to clear the forest and domesticate the wild as a foundational act to define progress. Nevertheless, there is an urgency to look back to nature with respect to heal the scars of industrialization.

The work compiled here tries to work with space in its pure form, and to explore its ultimate expressive possibilities by interacting in close proximity and intimacy with a strong natural environment. In addition to the cold tectonics of construction, prevalence is given to the poetics of pure form, twilight, mass and even the immaterial relationships which magically define a place and provide richness beyond pragmatic functionality.

Paul Cezanne
La Carrière de Bibémus, c. 1895
Museum Folkwang, Essen

Giovanni Battista Piranesi
View of the Cave Bergantino, 1762
National Gallery of Art, Washington DC (left)

Giovanni Battista Piranesi
The so-called Grotto of Egeria, ca. 1766
The Elisha Whittelsey Collection
The Metropolitan Museum of Art, NY

Space that Matters
by Rubén Alcolea

In 1762, Giovanni Battista Piranesi imagined an idealized version of Nymphaeum Bergantino, also known as the Baths of Diana, located only a few meters off the western shore of Lake Albano, in the municipality of Castel Gandolfo, Italy. The history of the caves dates back to 300 BC, and they were deliberately enlarged to be incorporated into Domitian's imperial villa in the first century. The space was both inhabited and forgotten intermittently for centuries. Even, it is said to have been used by Pope Alexander VII in the mid 1600s, and remaining well known at least by Piranesi during the mid 1700s. It was then forgotten again for a century until it was finally opened to public knowledge in the mid 1800s. The Nymphaeum was originally a pozzolan quarry with a few rooms, but was transformed into an excavated temple with magnificent floors covered by huge mosaics depicting sea creatures and walls covered with marble slabs and paintings. The interior space is, by far, quite smaller than as depicted by Piranesi, who idealized the space to adopt the majestic scale which its past was perhaps deserving. The rooms are depicted grandiose, truly deep, and fully inhabited. Although it suggests a semi-abandon status –as nature seems to want to take over the arch structures– the inhabitants roam around, mostly walking or standing in pairs, pointing to its wonders in all directions. The ruins certainly seduced Piranesi, who wondered what may have happened inside those carved rooms. The level of detail and the general proportions in his drawing suggest that he knew the place well. Nevertheless, the scale is amplified at least two or three times, enlarging the interior substantially. Natural light is also gently introduced through the sequence of rooms, suggesting impossible skylights or very high openings, in a dramatic and exaggeratedly profound central hall which seems to extend infinitely into the rock bed.

A few years later, Piranesi produced an etching of a similar space. On that occasion it was the so-called Nymphaeum of Egeria, an archeological structure still standing today, in the Appia Antica Regional Park. By detailed analysis of the scene, based on the principles of the perspective method and compared with the preserved Nymphaeum survey, it has been possible to identify the fundamental elements of the perspective. It is now geometrically proved that Piranesi manipulated not only the perspective, implementing operations which made the side wall less foreshortened but, ultimately, enlarged the vaults to recreate an amplified fiction of the original space.[1] As in the Baths of Diana, the Nymphaeum of Egeria is fully embedded in the mountain, an effect which is also stressed in the etching. The distortion of scale is exaggerated to make it look more magnificent. To Piranesi's eyes, it adopts a scale closer to the Baths at Caracalla rather to the relatively small grotto. Beyond its morphology, what seems relevant –at least to Piranesi's eyes– is that both spaces are fully carved, a sort of anti-building, conceived and created by pure subtraction of its inhabitable space. In addition to trying to simply render the construction, Piranesi embraced the concept of depicting a humanized and architecturally intellectualized cave, connecting with the idealized structures of splendorous ancient times. The possibility of redefining the existing place and considering it as a starting point to further investigate on the idea of a fully carved space, is what ultimately made both etchings so magic.

The track of humans inhabiting caves is extensive and dates to prehistoric times, but those pragmatic appropriations of already existing spaces as a shelter are different to what Piranesi is suggesting through these idealized versions. On both occasions, the original cave is transformed into a well-tempered interior, a sort of sculptured surface which gently wraps an atmosphere, a place. In addition to the intrinsic qualities of the space itself, Piranesi embellishes the scene with exuberant nature taking over the ruins, creating an ambiguous recreation, still artificial but substantially natural. A new scene in which nature and architecture tradition could try to dialogue in pure spatial terms. Up to that moment, buildings and architecture had generally been understood in terms of additive construction, in which space is the result of enclosing voids through surfaces or architecture elements –such as columns, walls, ceilings or floors–, and engaging in different levels of complexity but according to strict composition rules. The possibility of an architecture built from the inside, by literally carving the inhabited space, and denying any chance of external representativity, points to a new interpretation of how buildings could be defined. It even questions if spaces such as the Nymphaeum Bergantino or at Egeria are themselves buildings as such; and opens the door to engage in redefining the classic notion of architecture.

What, then, is architecture? And, perhaps equally important, what is this non-architecture? These same questions were already stated in the prologue "Architecture, the unknown" in Bruno Zevi's *Architecture as Space*.[2] There is a certain agreement that "space" is somehow the protagonist of architecture, evolving from the classic conceptualization of architecture as the arrangement of mostly bidimensional elements. In his seminal text, Zevi eloquently points to a new way of interpreting classic or ancient architecture, far beyond its pure historic or stylistic aspects, but identifying the quest for pure space as a true invention. The text has been widely referenced, specially when Zevi points out that "the most exact definition of architecture can be given today is that which takes into account interior space".[3] Other studies have followed elaborating on similar ideas, referring to the three distilled concepts of space enunciated originally by Albert Brinckmann in 1908: firstly, the freestanding sculptural mass surrounded by space; secondly, space surrounded by mass; and thirdly the culmination, i.e. the interpenetration of the first two, as they exist in the Baroque and Rococo interiors.[4] Cornelis Van der Ven mentions it directly in his book *Space in Architecture*,[5] in a clear example that Brinckmann has influenced every major narrative addressing how space is interpreted through the twentieth century, including Zevi's or the volume *Space, Time and Architecture* by Siegfried Giedion.[6]

In that sense, the Nympheums by Piranesi are perhaps a perfect example of that so-called "culmination" of space, in which the freestanding sculptural mass is directly –and only– surrounded by the space it creates. Many historic sites and temples, such as the Ajanta and Elephanta Caves in India; the Lycian tombs in Turkey; or the astonishing temples at Petra in Jordan, address that direct notion of building by carving. The famous Chand Boari step wells in North India, for example, define an inverted empty pyramid carved in the ground, accessed through the top to then spiral down deep into the earth. But beyond those and many other ancient examples, it is difficult to find modern cases in which a traditional building is only perceived through its interior space. That could only be possible by lacking an exterior facade, substituting it with its interior as its major and only representation.

On that regard, the Pantheon of Agrippa in Rome is a good example, although its strong urban condition makes it impossible to be defined only by its interior. And although not a purely carved space, Bernini's Sant'andrea al Quirinale (1658-1670) gets close to become a full synthetic effect. Many other expressionist examples, such as the work by Rudolf Steiner, Frederick Kiesler, or even some unbuilt projects by Jørn Utzon, suggest the possibility of an architecture purely expressed and perceived through its interior. Many contemporary examples deal with this condition, but mainly through interventions in the interior of relatively large container buildings, in which the definition of the space is closer to becoming just a thin surface, a sort of theatrical stage, and generally lacking the density and thickness provided by the weight of truly carved soil or matter, present in all those historic projects. But all of them, nevertheless, cannot avoid the reality of having to deal with an exterior expression of its volumetry, which necessarily challenges the pure interior-only project. In any case, all have in common a substantial negation of the traditional concept of facade and composition, which undoubtedly forces us to rethink how the ideal space should be designed. It allows the opportunity to shortcut into working with pure voids and define how they are perceived both visually but also haptically. When there is nothing more than space defined by a carved and extended surface or material, every subtle variation becomes intensely major, and sensuality overcomes any possible intellectualized approach to the discipline. In addition to basic concepts or strategies, always inevitably present, is now pure matter what matters.

1. Menconero, Sofia. "Piranesi at the Nymphaeum of Egeria: Perspective Expedients." In *Graphical Heritage, Representation, Analysis, Concept and Creation*, edited by Luis Agustín Hernández, Aurelio Vallespín Muniesa, and Angélica Fernández-Morales, 6:343–56. EGA. Cham: Springer, 2020.

2. Zevi, Bruno. *Architecture as Space: How to Look at Architecture*. New York: Horizon Press, 1957, 24.

3. Zevi, Bruno, op. Cit., 28.

4. Brinckmann, Albert Erich. *Platz Und Monument. Untersuchungen Zur Geschichte Und Aesthetik Der Stadtbgaukunst in Neueren Zeit*. 1908. Reprint, Berlin: Wasmuth, 1923, 208.

5. Van de Ven, Cornelis. *Space in Architecture: The Evolution of a New Idea in the Theory and History of the Modern Movements*. Assen: Van Gorcum, 1978, 113.

6. Giedion, Sigfried. *Space, Time and Architecture: The Growth of a New Tradition*. 1941. Reprint, Cambridge, Mass.: Harvard University Press, 1967.

No. 85.—Freedley's Marble Quarry.

Freedley's Quarry in Dorset, VT
Current Status, 2021 (left)

Freedley's Quarry in Dorset, VT
Stereoscopic Photography, C1850

Part One
Hypogeans d'Invenzione

Planar representations and abstract drawings provide a valuable source for defining generative spaces. Historically, architecture has navigated through a balancing act of dealing with mass and void, heaviness and lightness, density and porosity. Scrutinizing historic interventions provides a valuable source for understanding the principle to rule those concepts. The analysis of the projects and their scale –which range from rooms to the landscape and territory– allows to generate abstract and open-ended drawings which. That is the starting point to idealize a carved space with no particular scale, program or materiality. The spaces are then being translated into volumetric models which will accentuate non physical elements such as thresholds and twilight, pointing to an idealized and non-scalar project.

The reference projects studied are grandiose and timeless in their architecture strategy. The list is long, and refert to places such as the Ajanta Caves, Aurangabad, India; Elephanta Caves, Elephanta Island, Maharashtra, India Varaha Cave Temple, Tamil Nadu, India; Chand Bahori, Bandikui, India; Kailasa Temple, Ellora, India; Church of Saint George, Lalibela, Ethiopia; Phraya Nakhon Temple, Sam Roi You, Thailand; San Juan De la Peña Monastery, Spain; Holy Kipinas Monastery, Kalarrites, Greece; Hermitage of Saint Sava, Savovo, Serbia; Predjama Castle, Slovenia; Kropfenstein Castle, Waltensburg, Switzerland; Ruine Puxer-Loch, Styria, Austria; Rappenstein Castle, Untervaz, Switzerland; Lycian Tombs, Fethiye, Turkey; Sigiriya, Sri Lanka; Petra, Ma'an Governorate, Jordan; Longmen Grottoes, Luoyang, Henan, China; and Bamiyan Buddhas, Afghanistan.

Kailasa Temple
Ellora - Kailasanatha, India
Photo by Anwar Nillufany

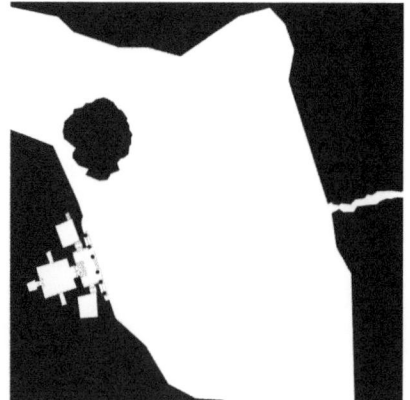

Petra, Ma'an Governorate, Jordan

Kropfenstein Castle, Waltensburg, Switzerland

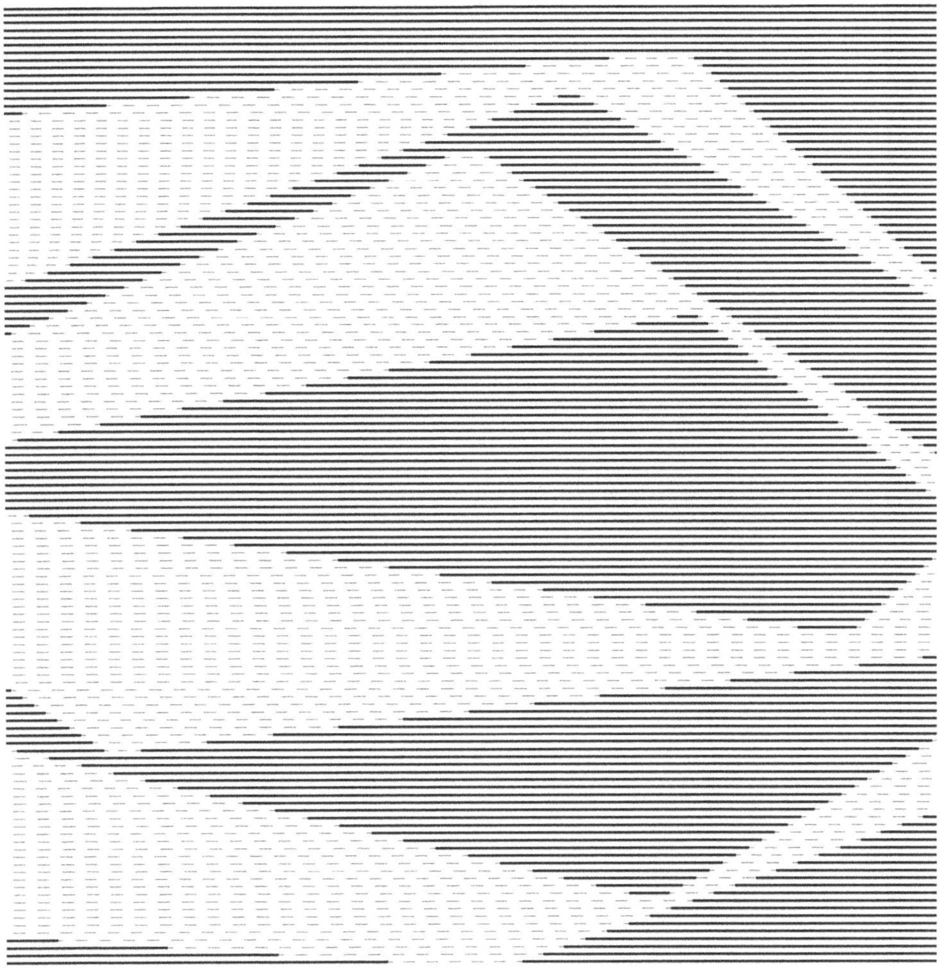

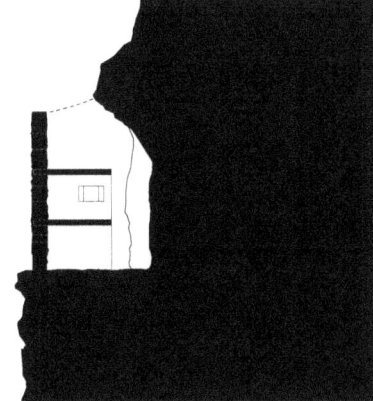

Lycian Tombs, Fethiye, Turkey

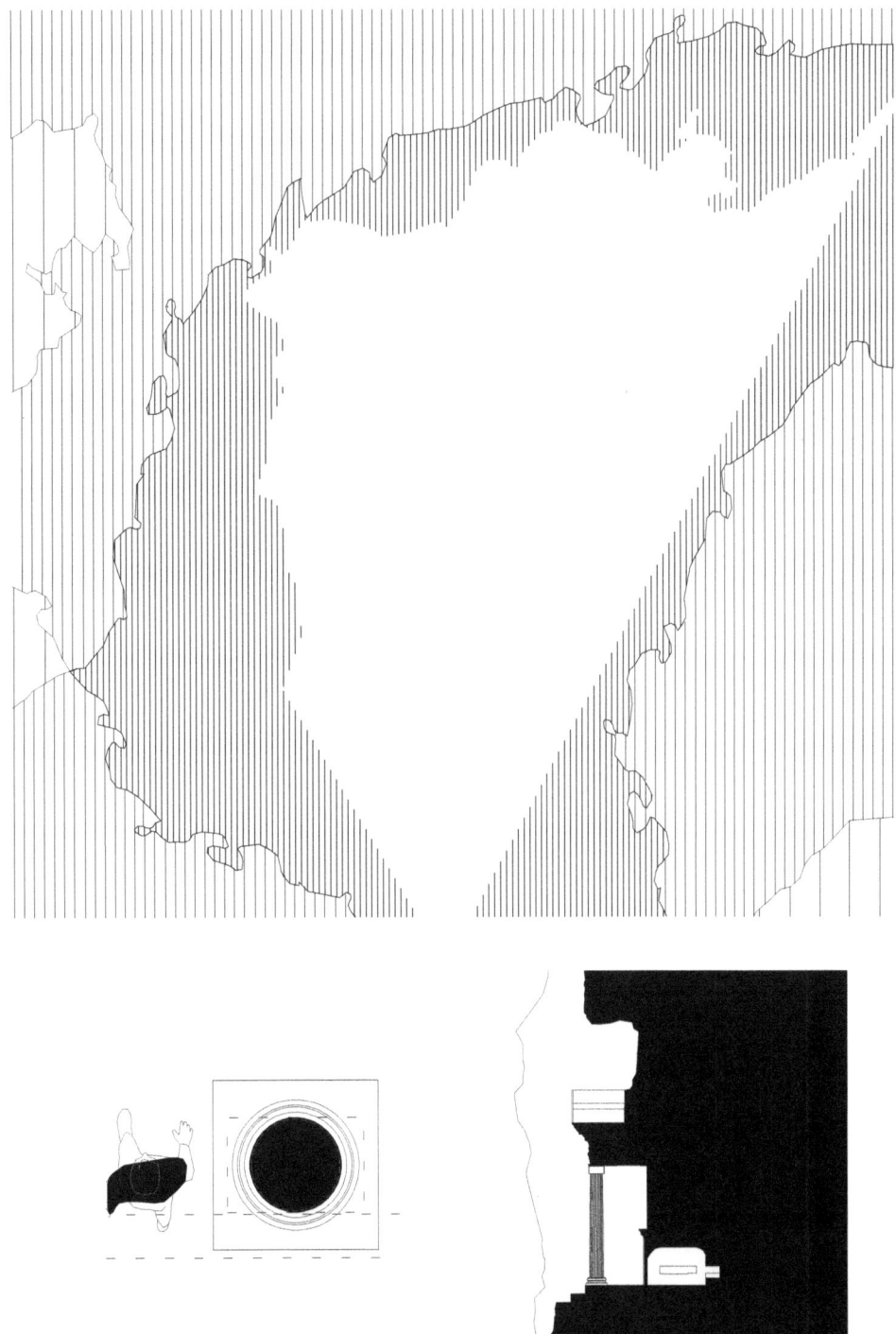

 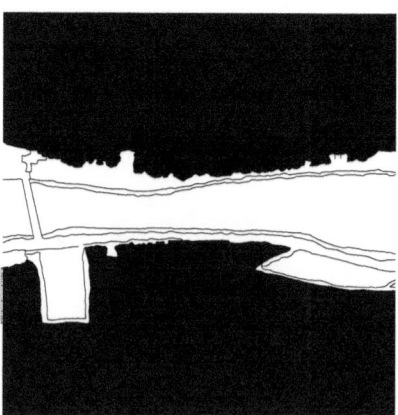

Longmen Grottoes, Luoyang, Henan, China

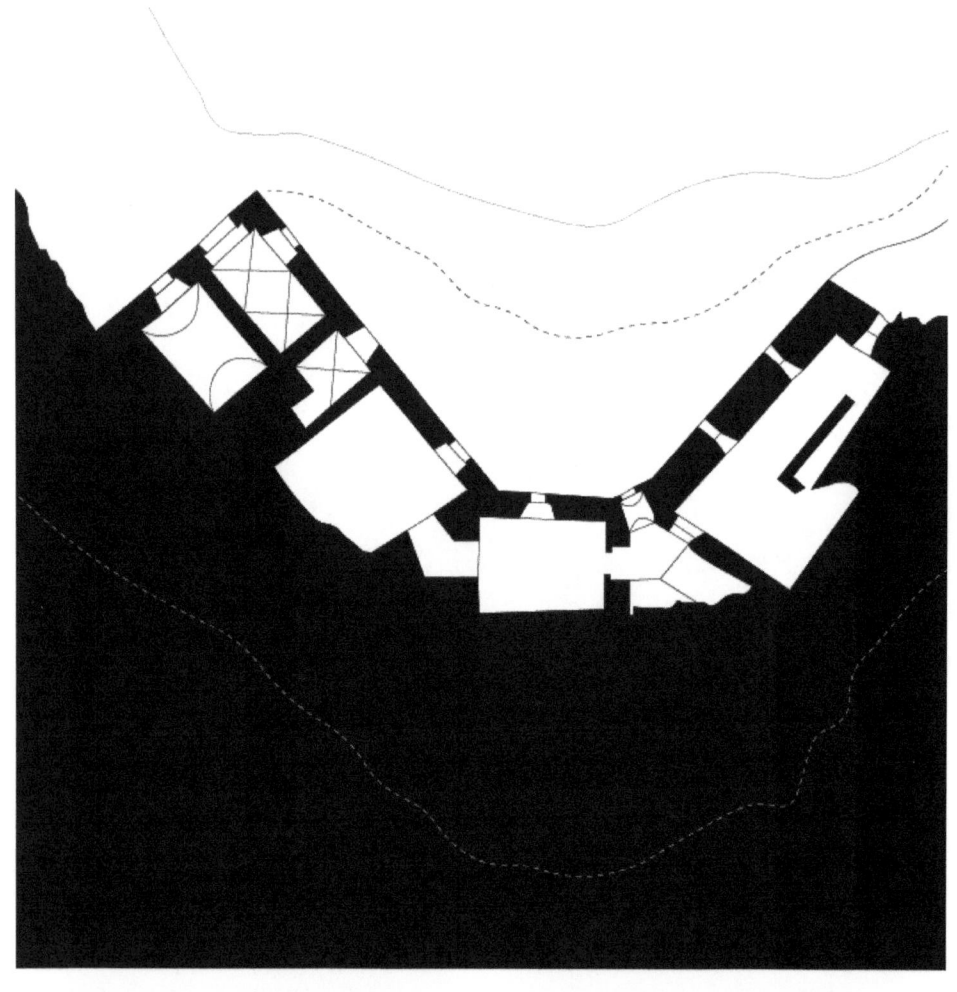

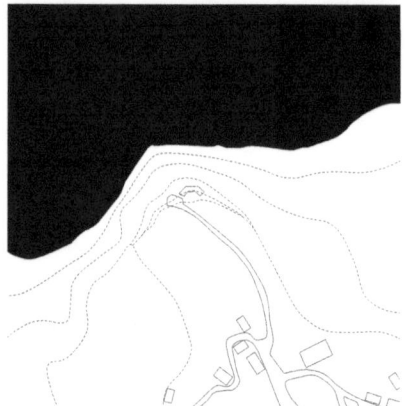

Predjama Castle, Slovenia

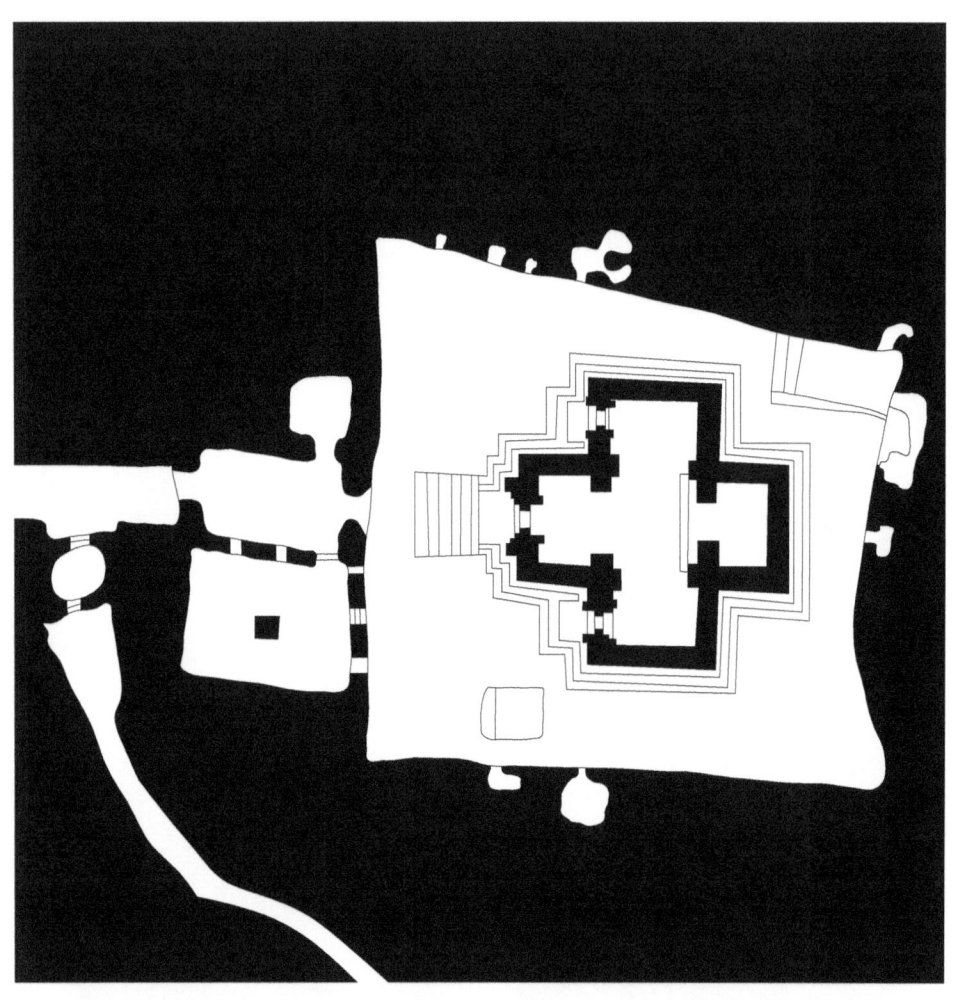

 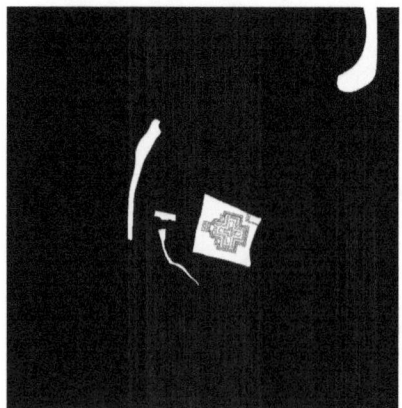

Church of Saint George, Lalibela, Ethiopia

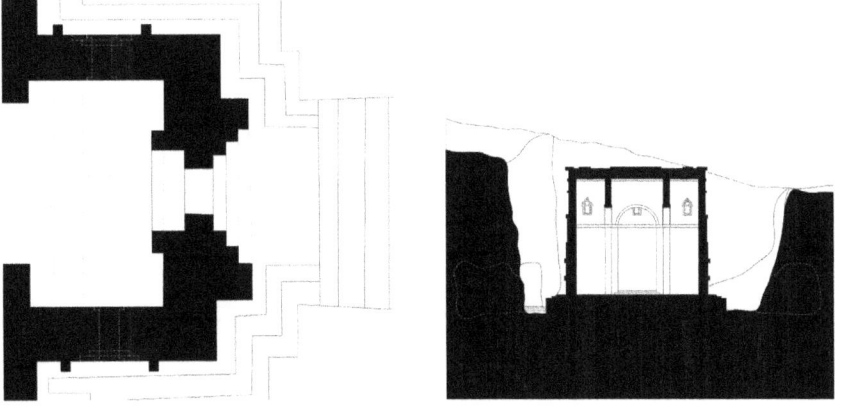

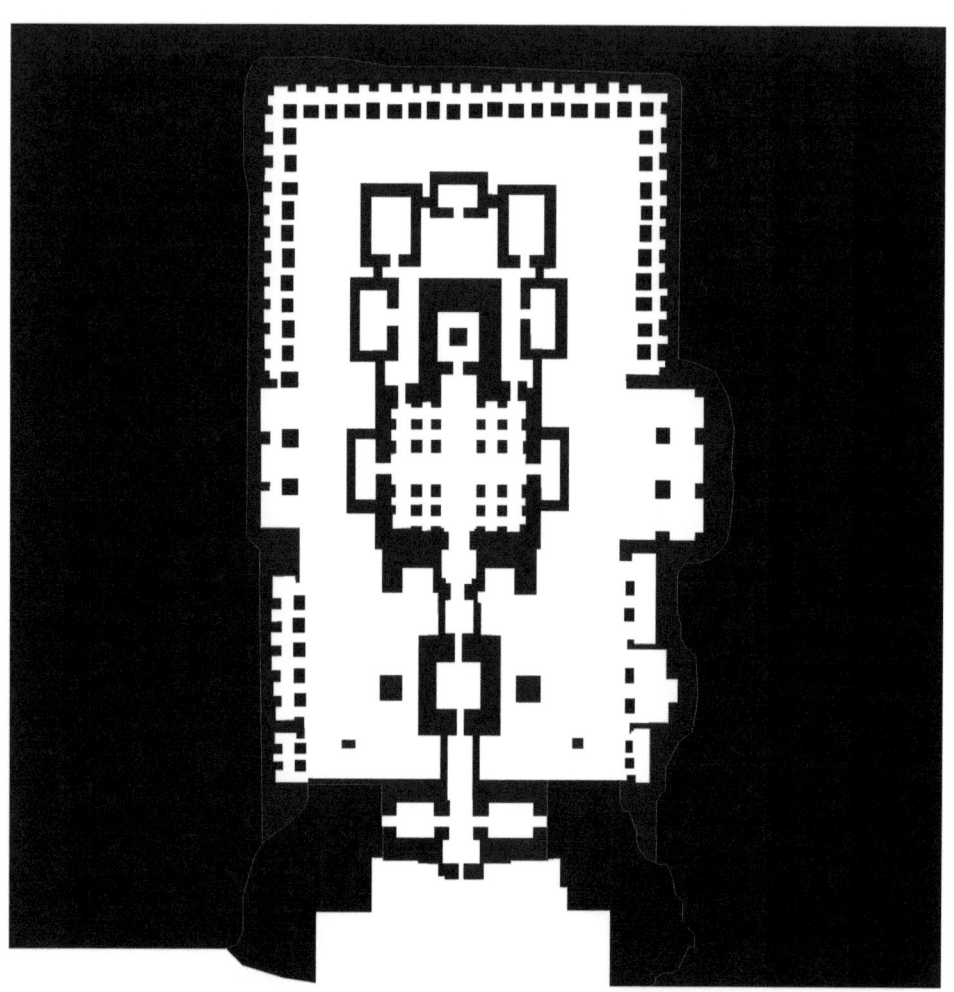

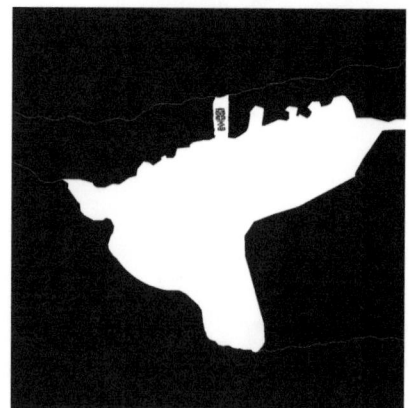

Kailasa Temple, Ellora, India

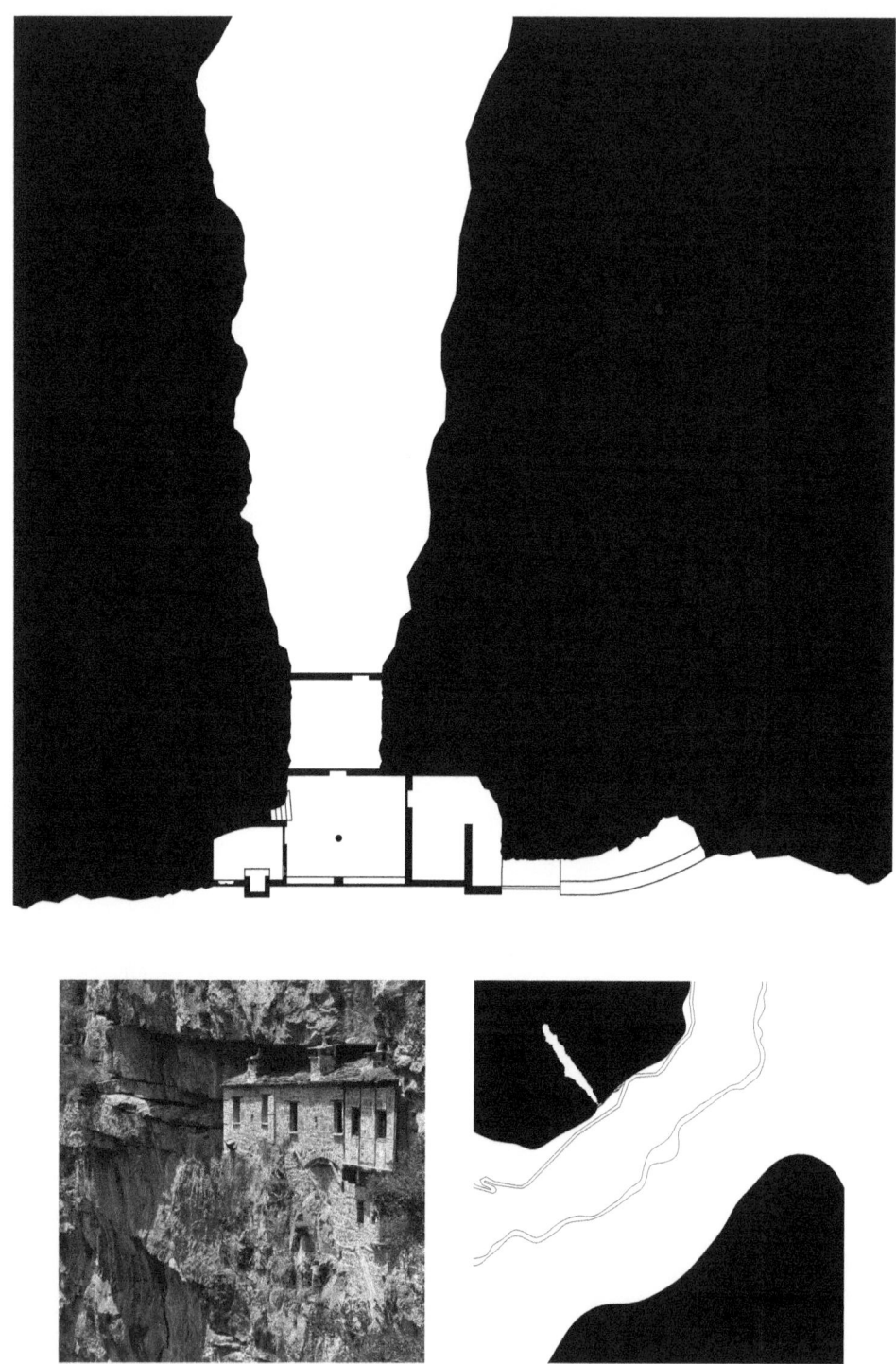

Holy Kipinas Monastery, Kalarrites, Greece

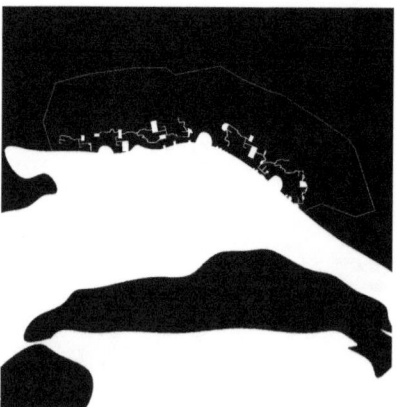

Bamiyan Buddhas, Afghanistan

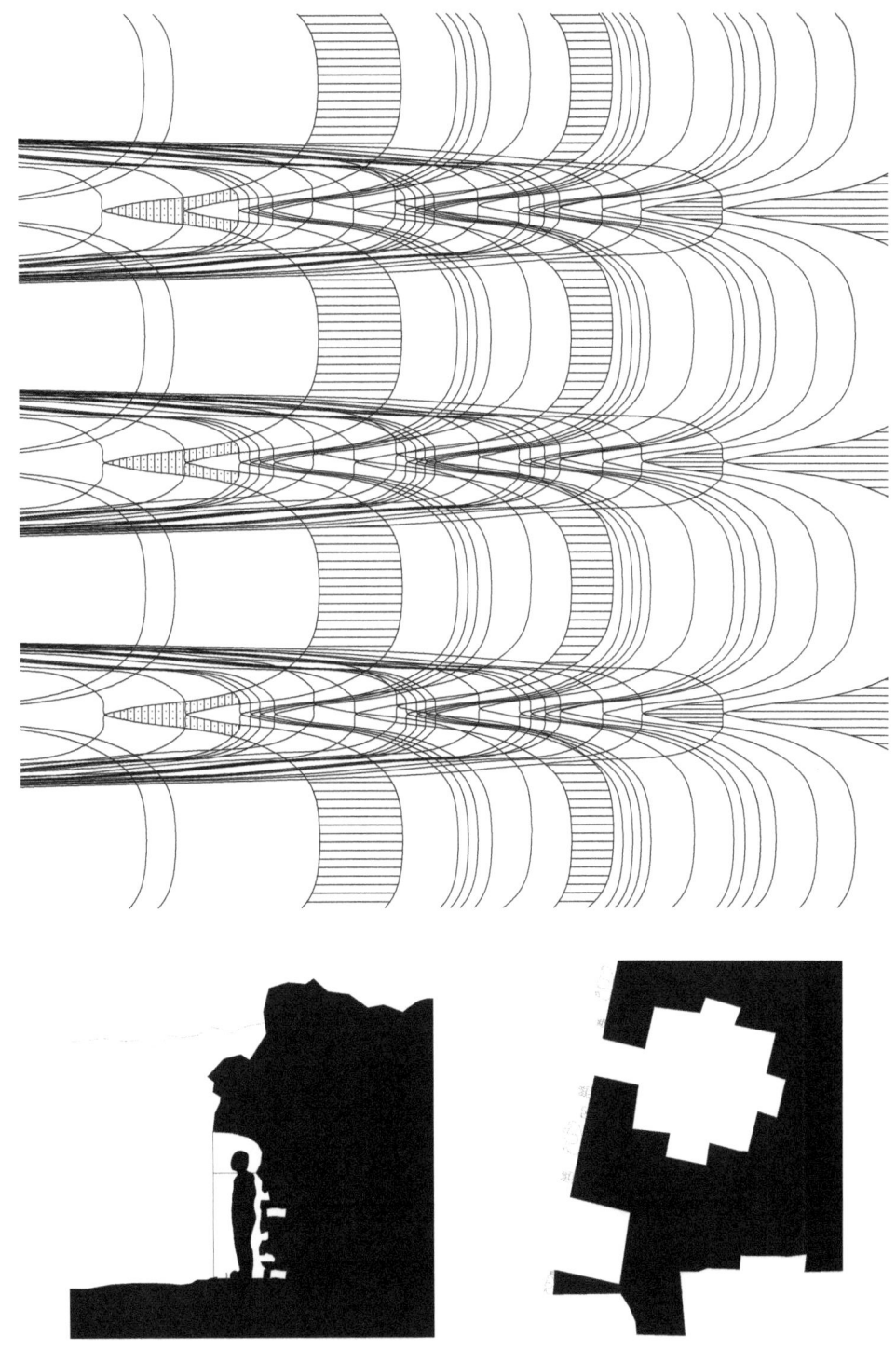

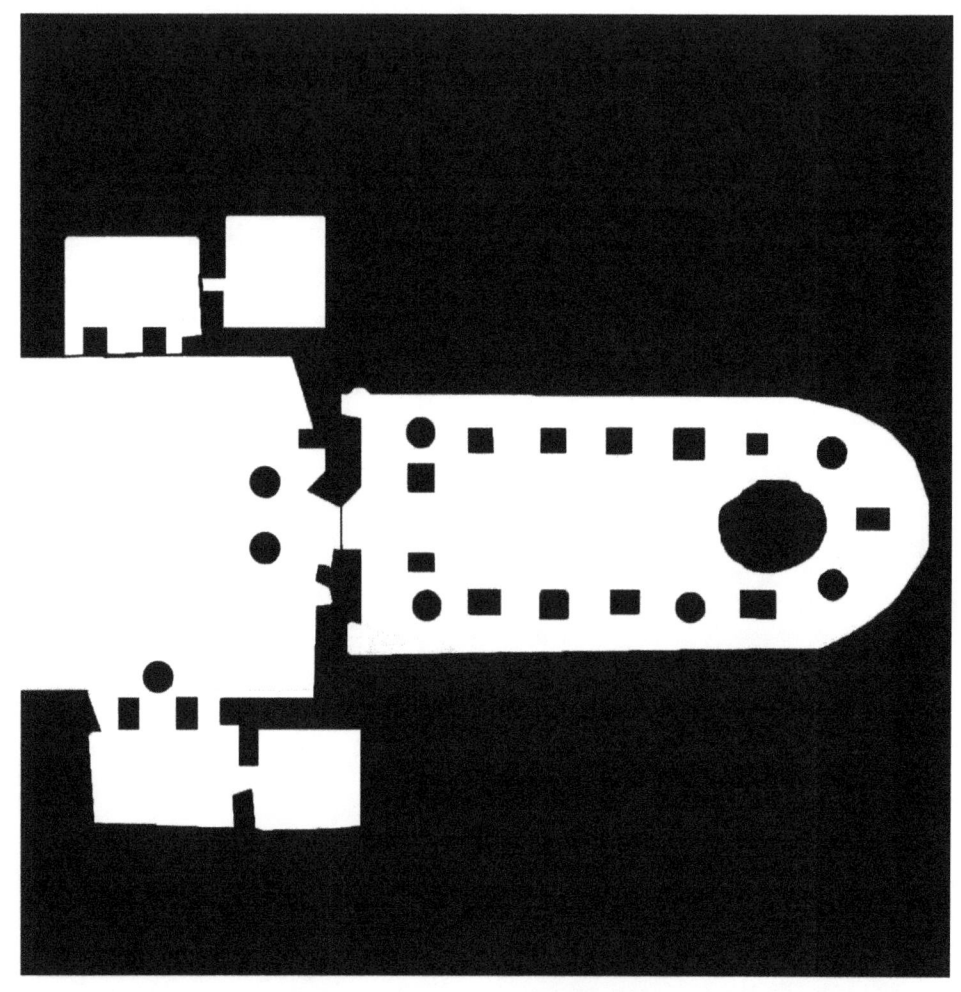

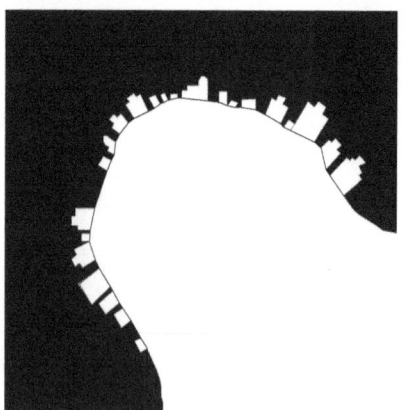

Ajanta Caves, Aurangabad, India

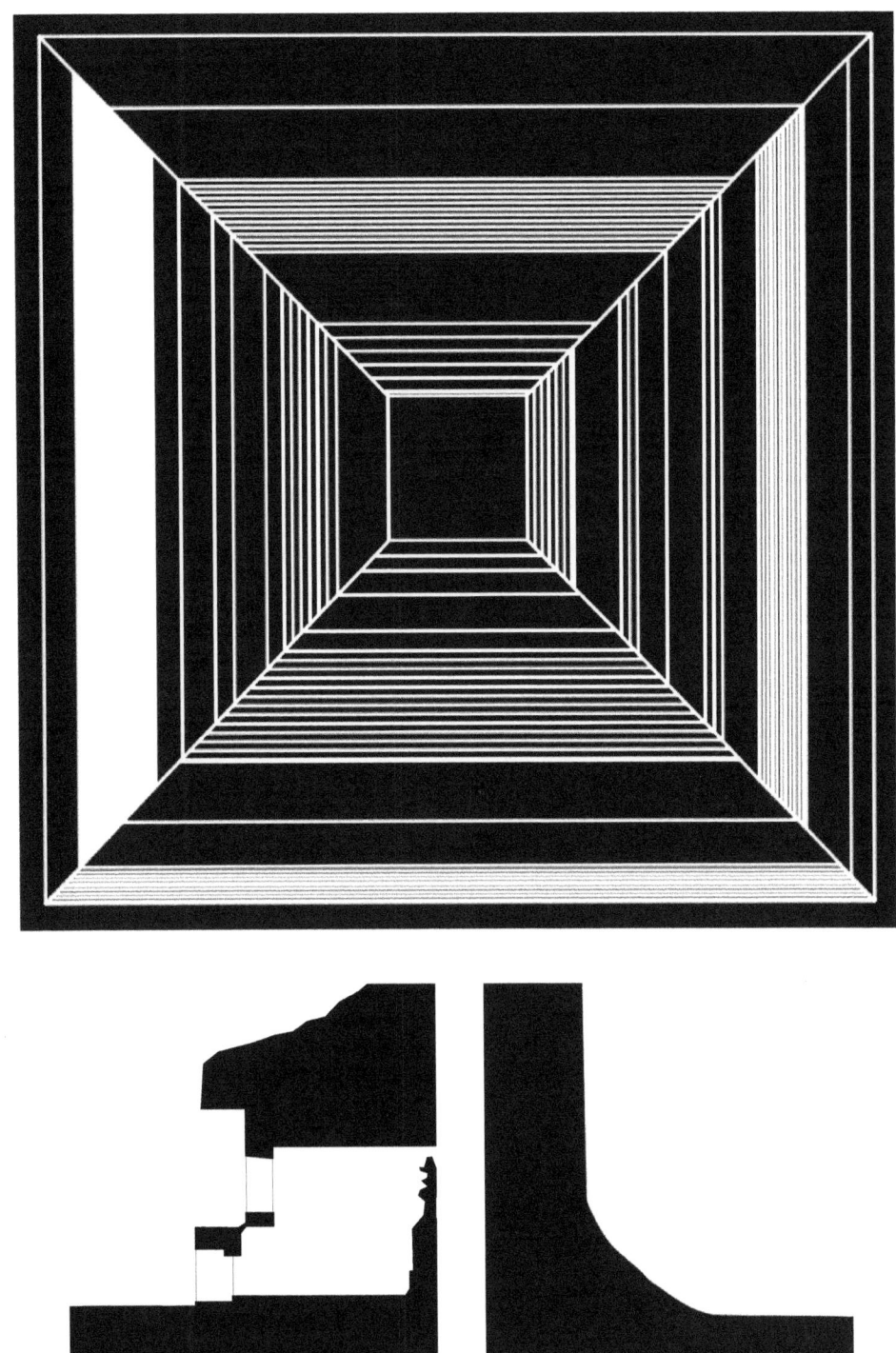

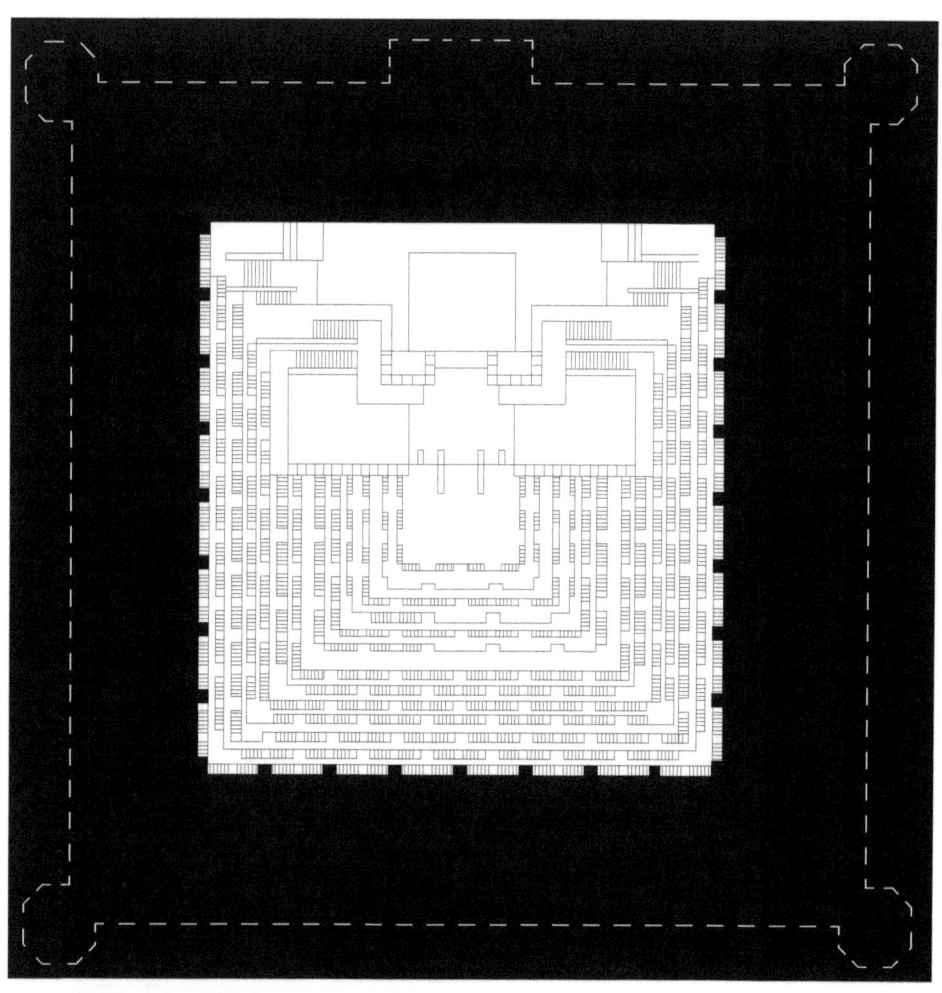

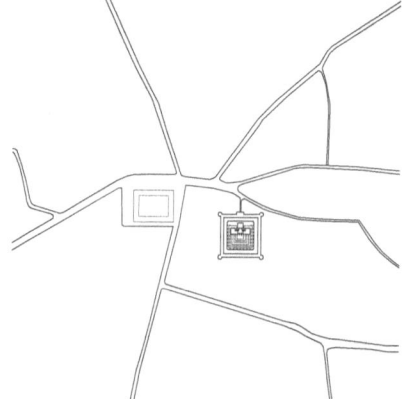

Chand Bahori, Bandikui, India

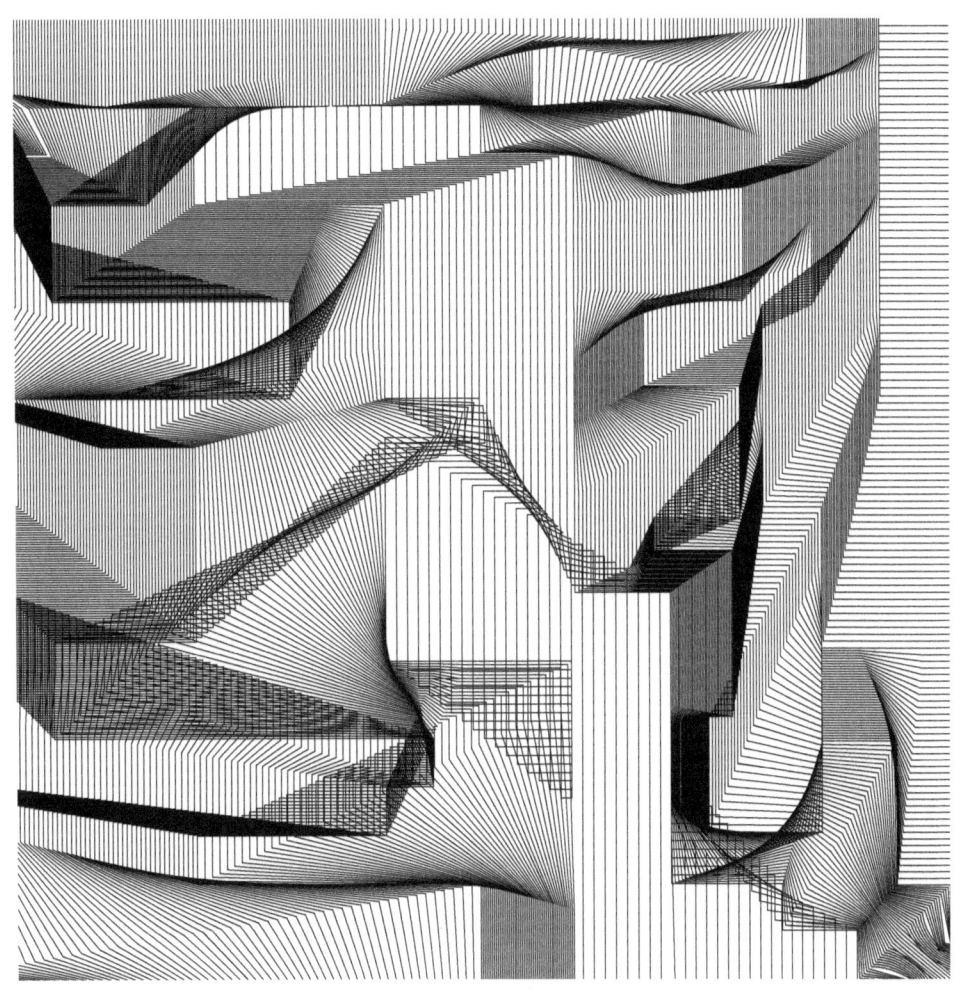

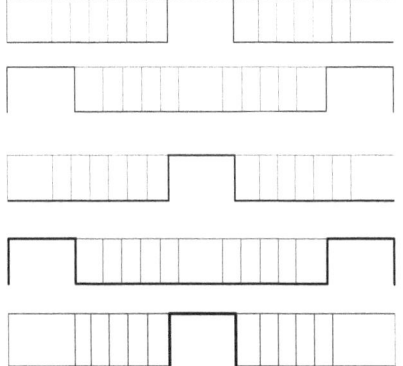

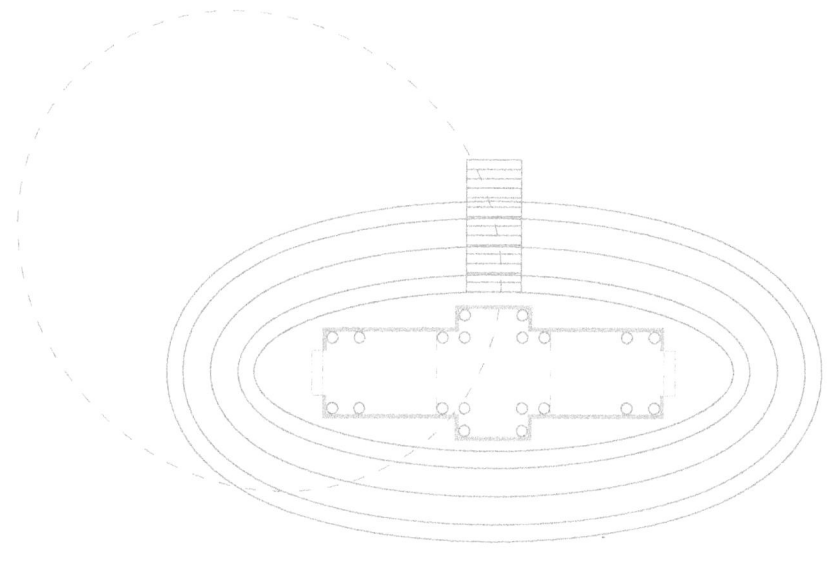

Phraya Nakhon Temple, Sam Roi You, Thailand

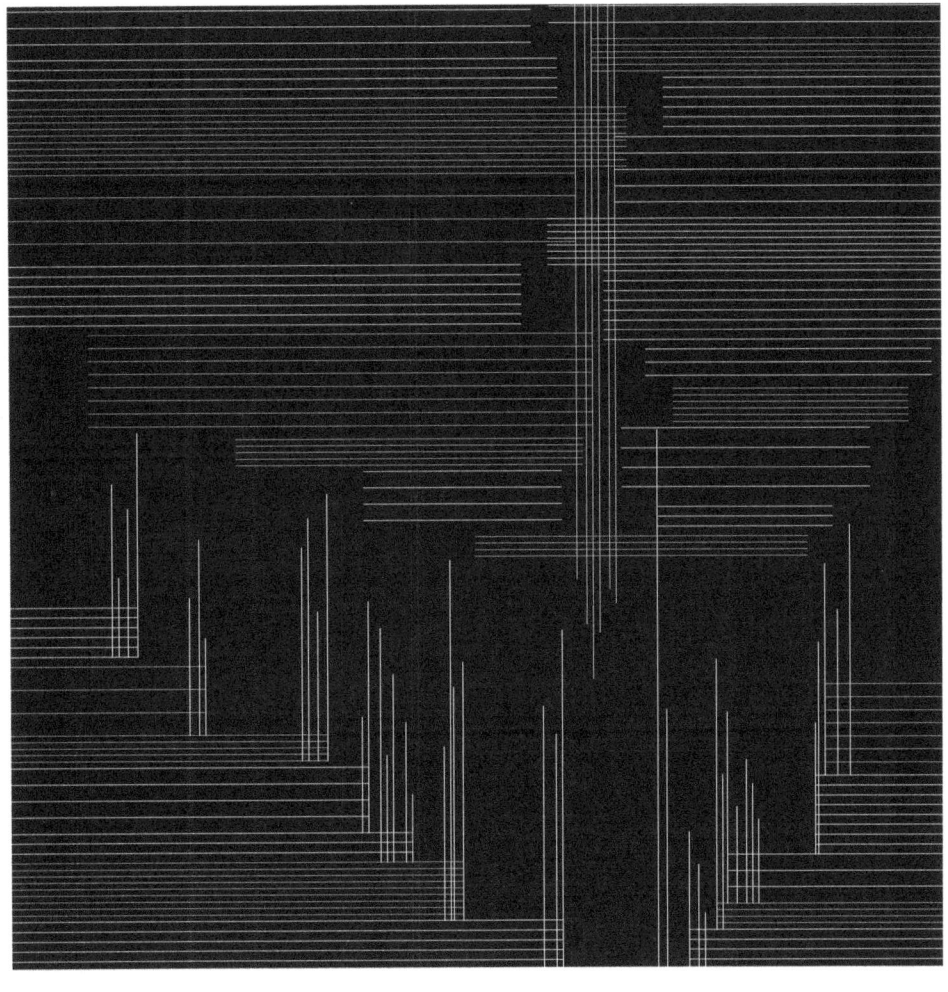

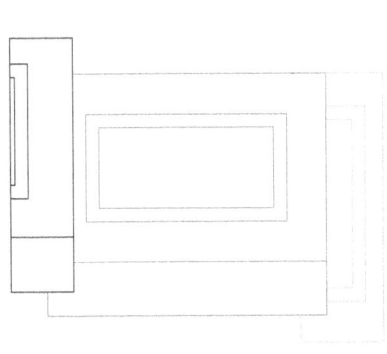

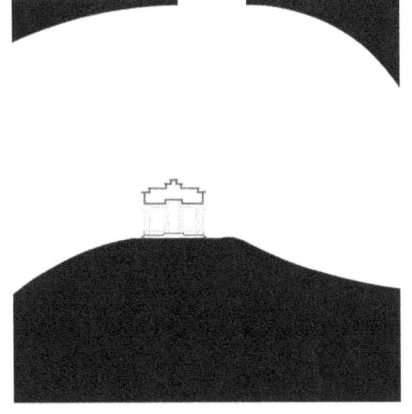

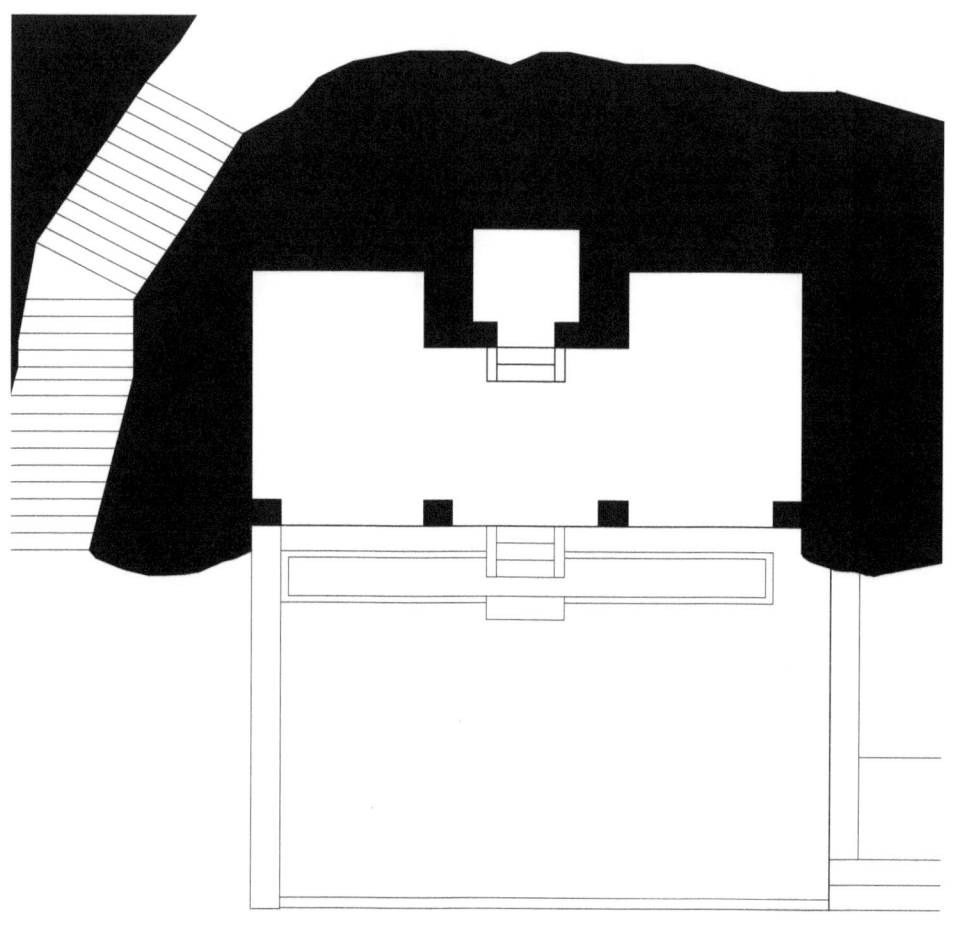

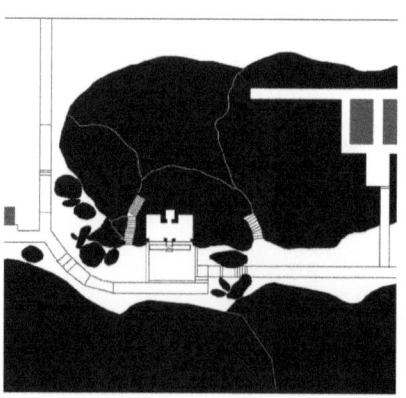

Varaha Cave Temple, Tamil Nadu, India

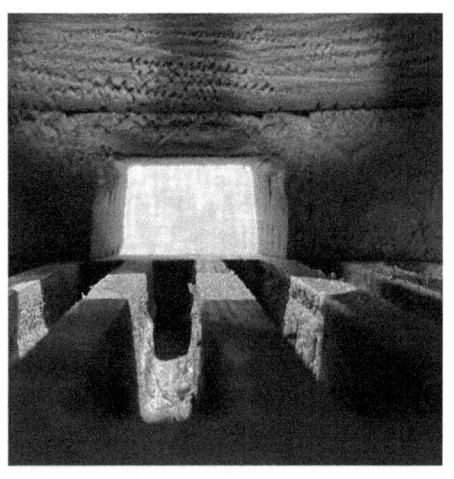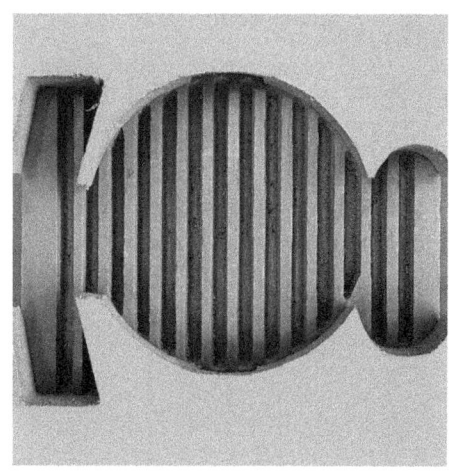

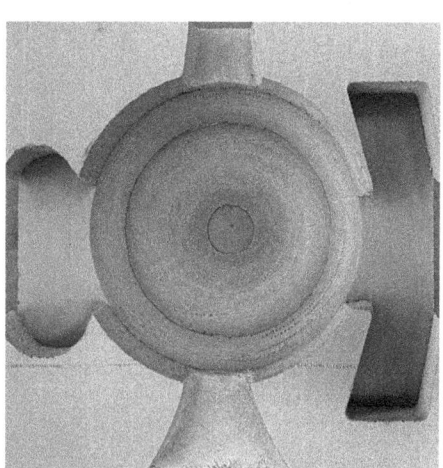

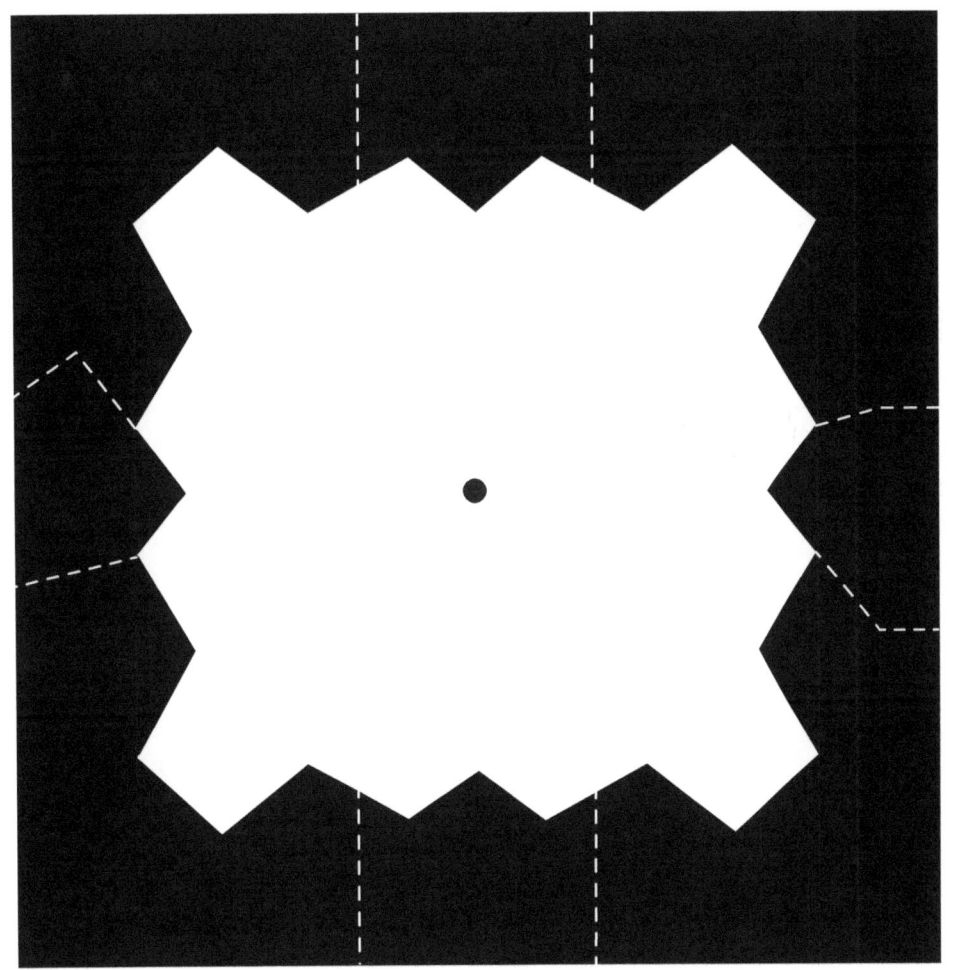

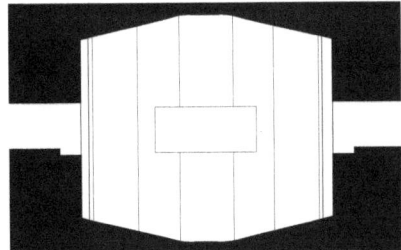 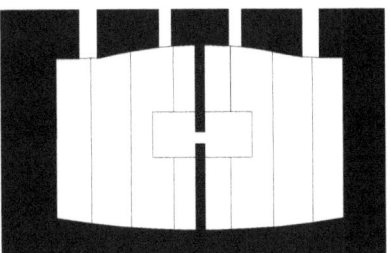

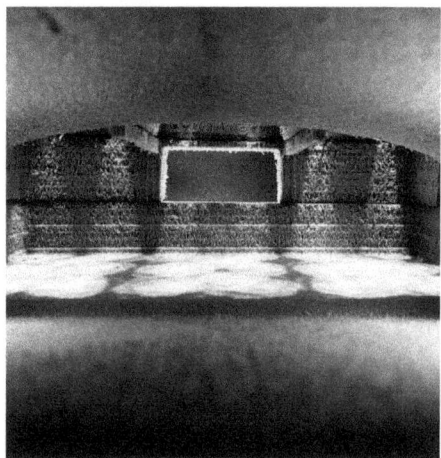
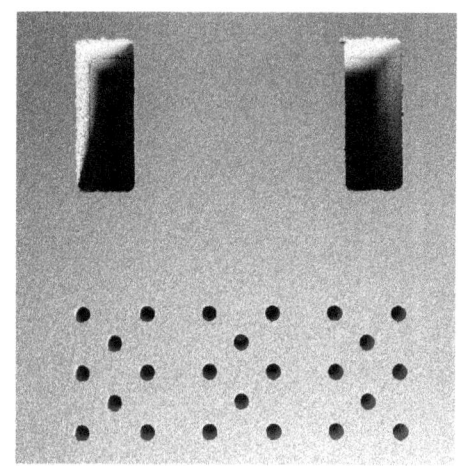

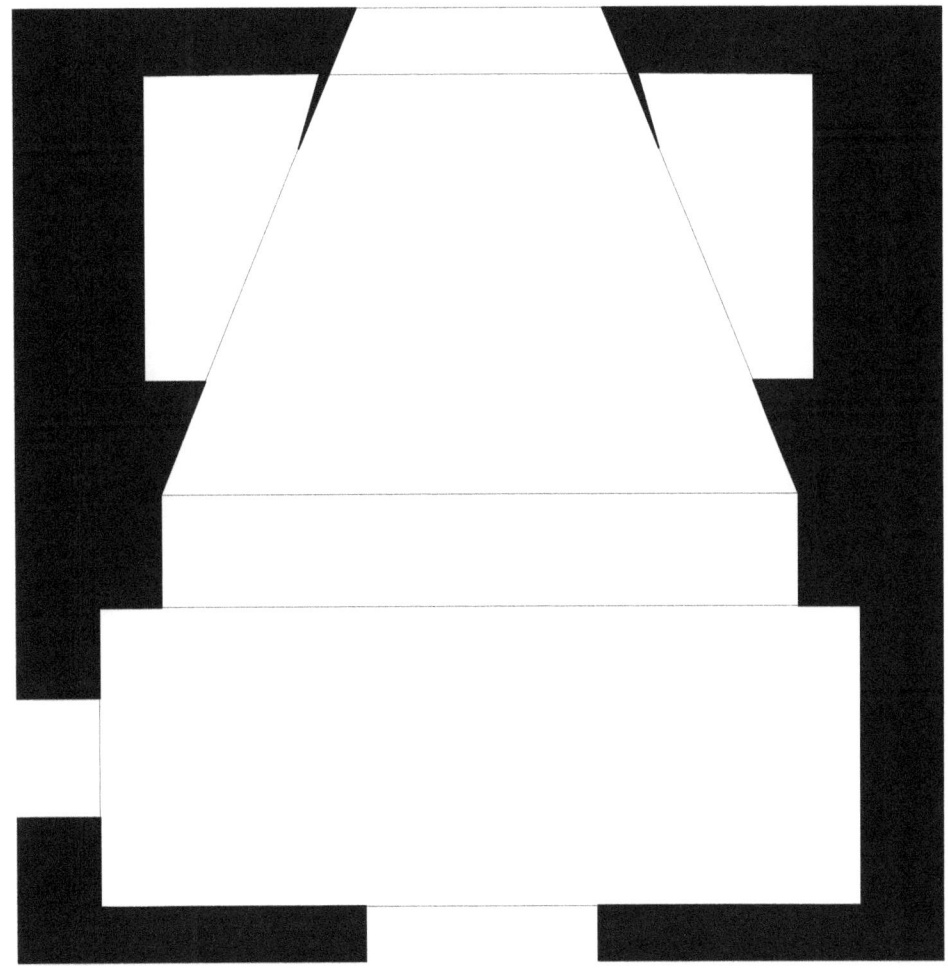

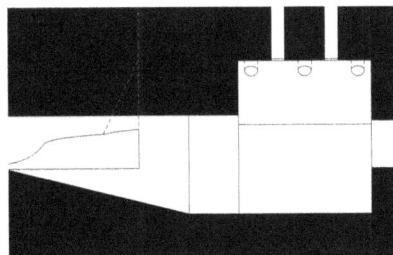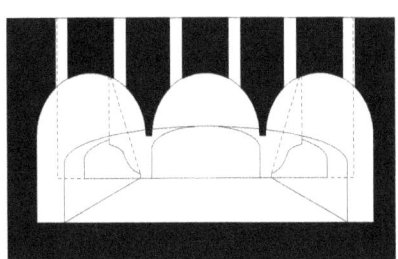

 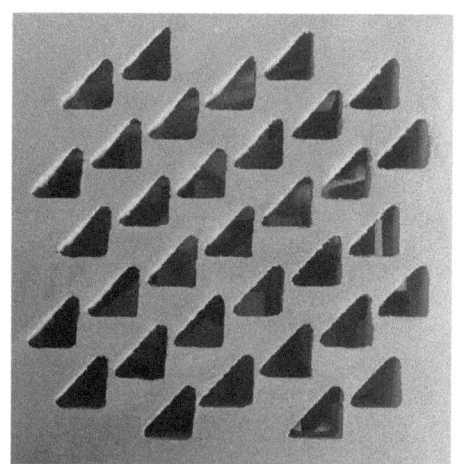

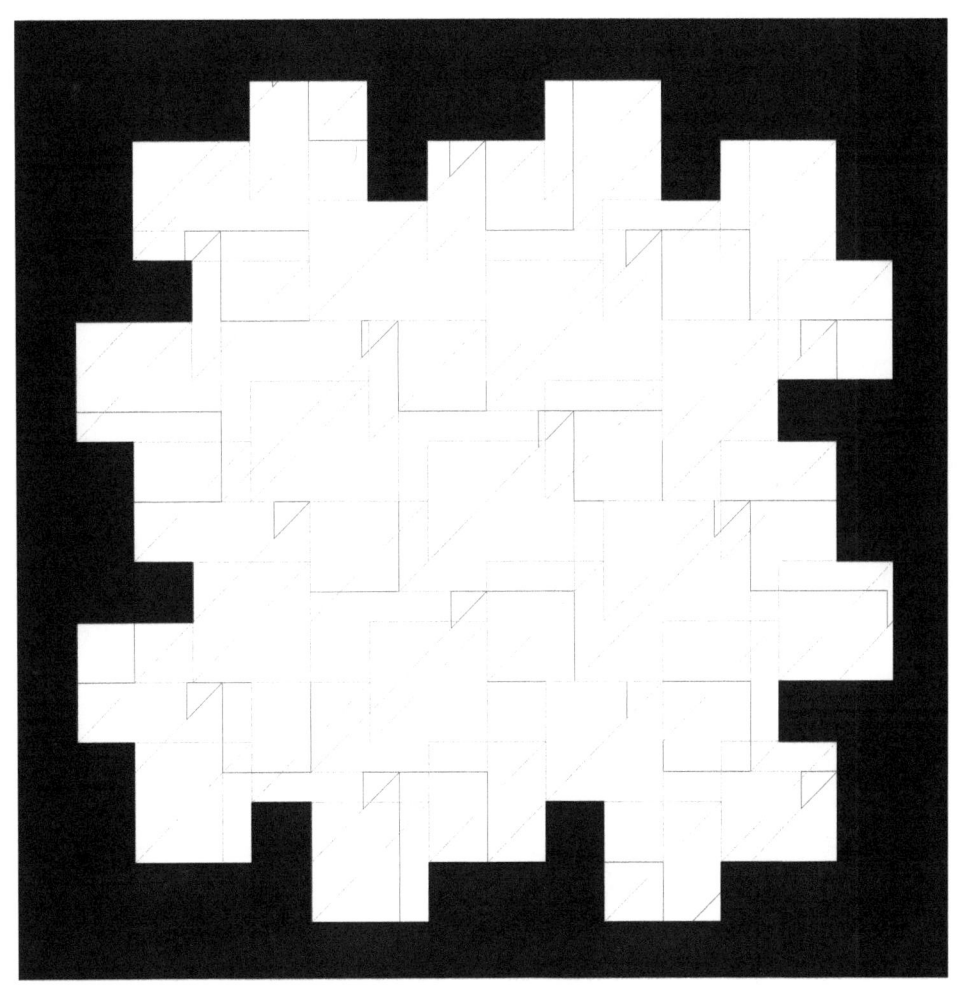

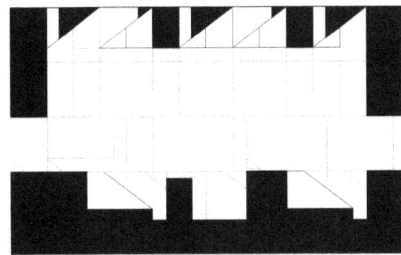
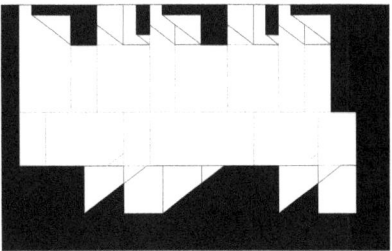

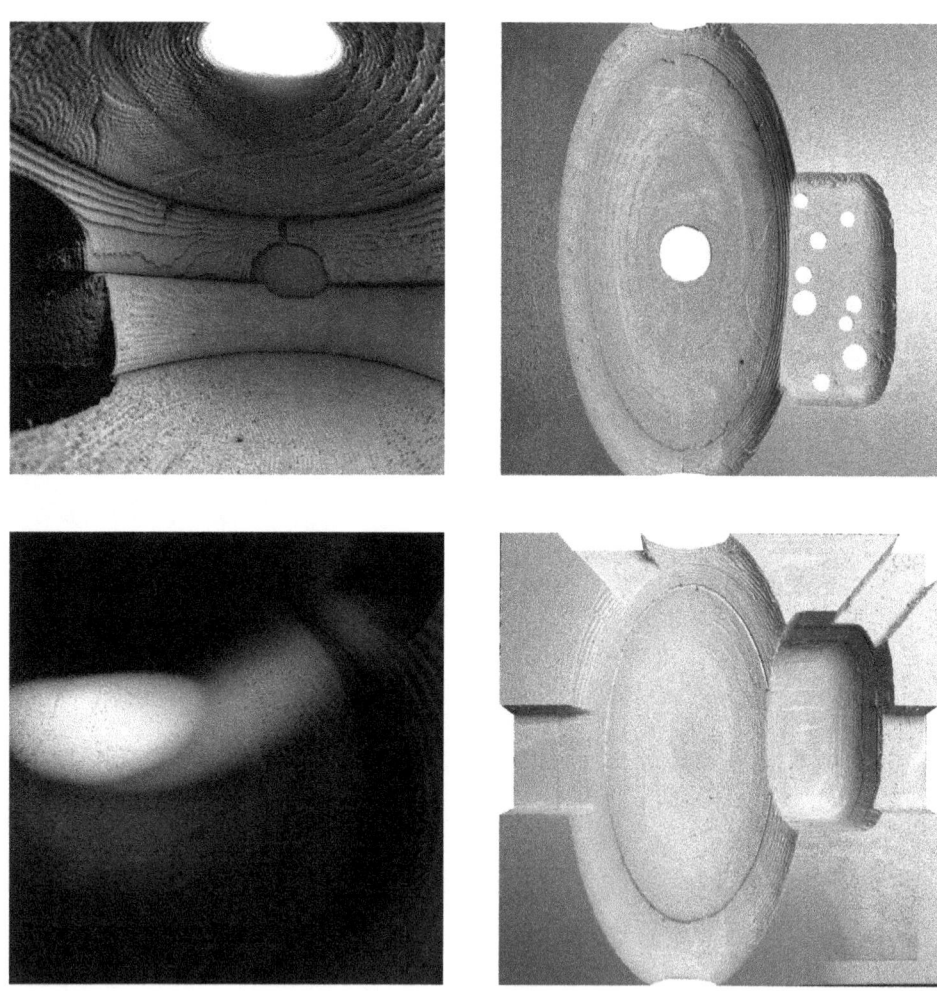

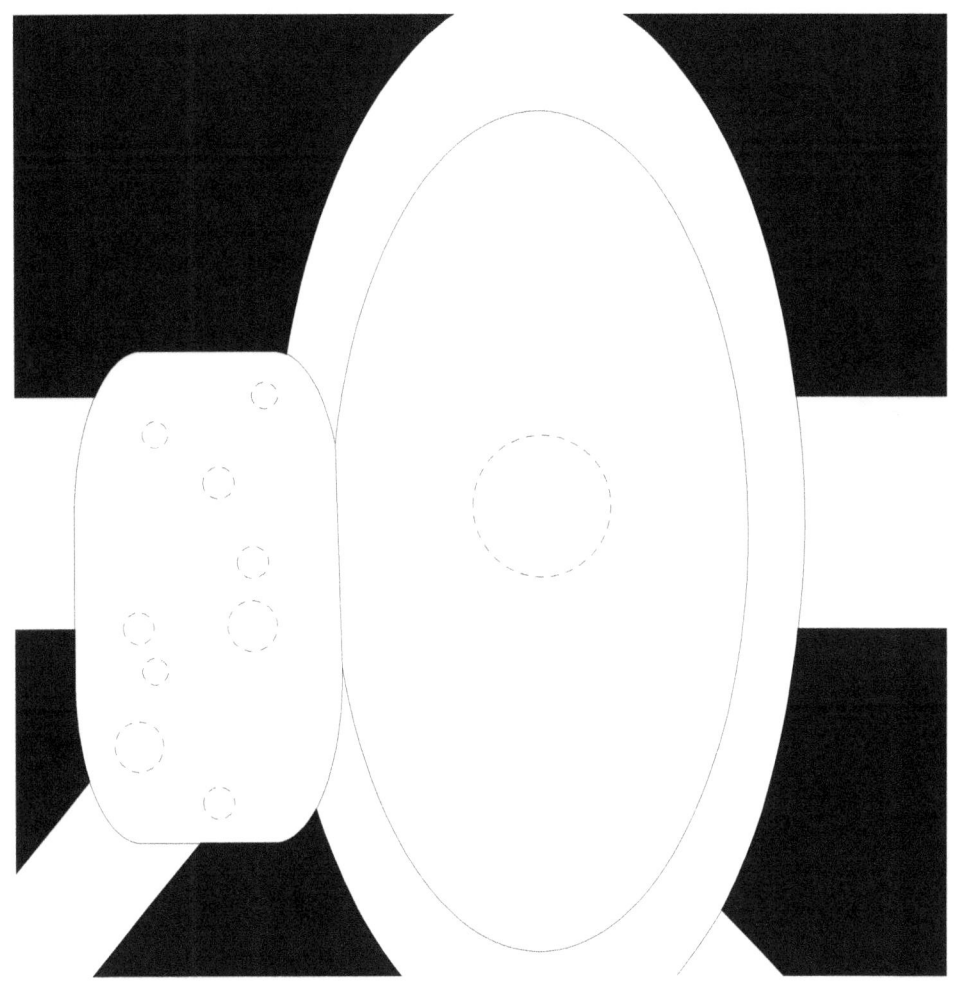

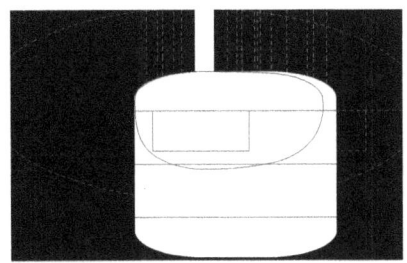
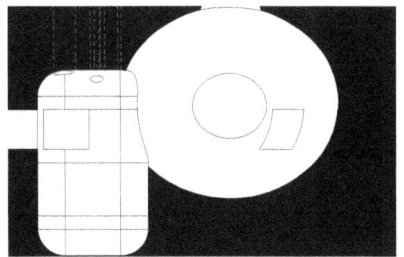

 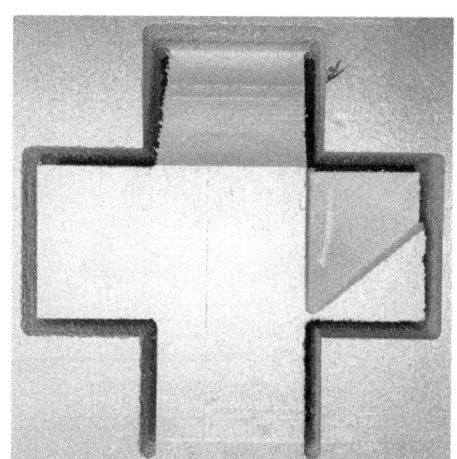

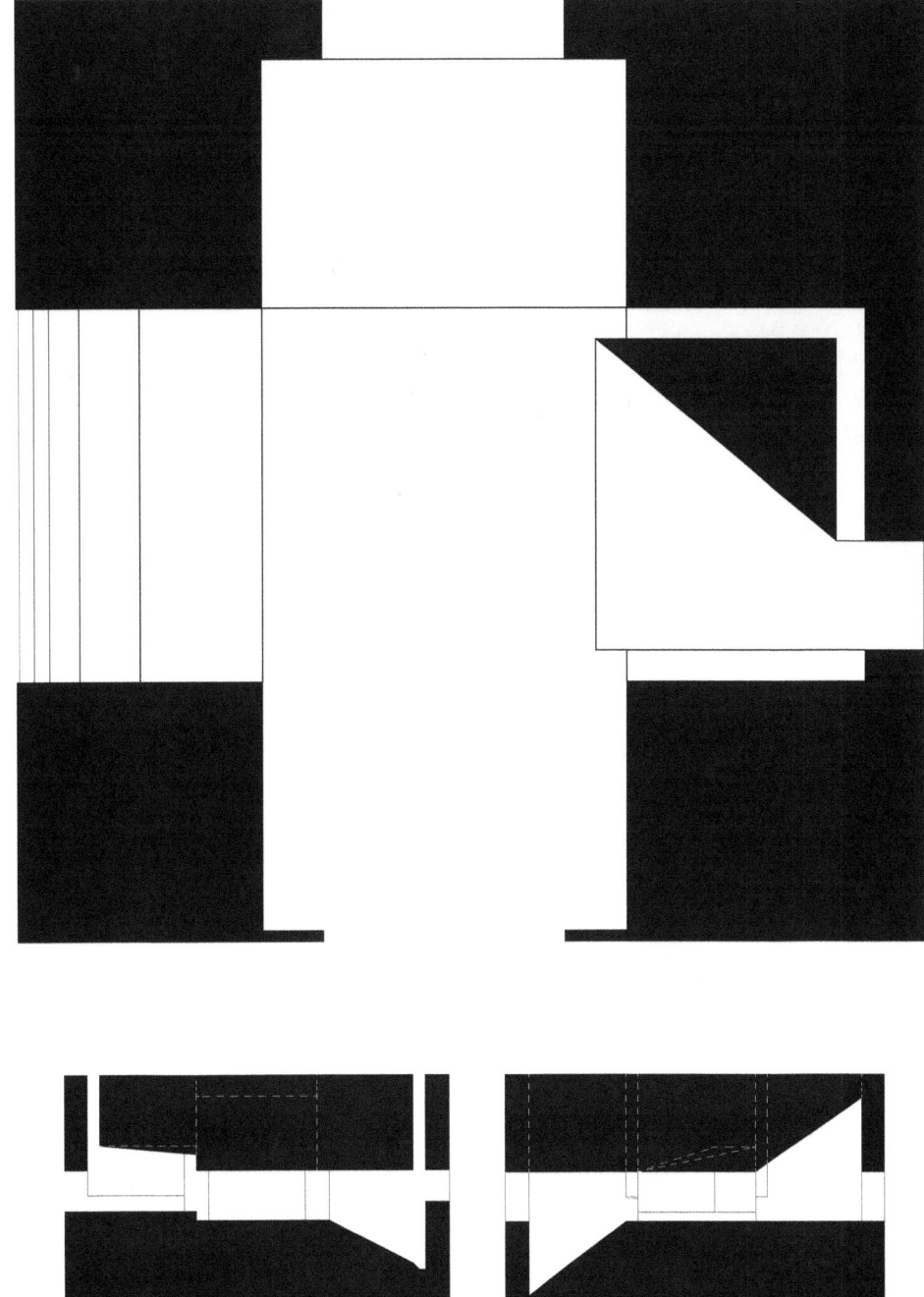

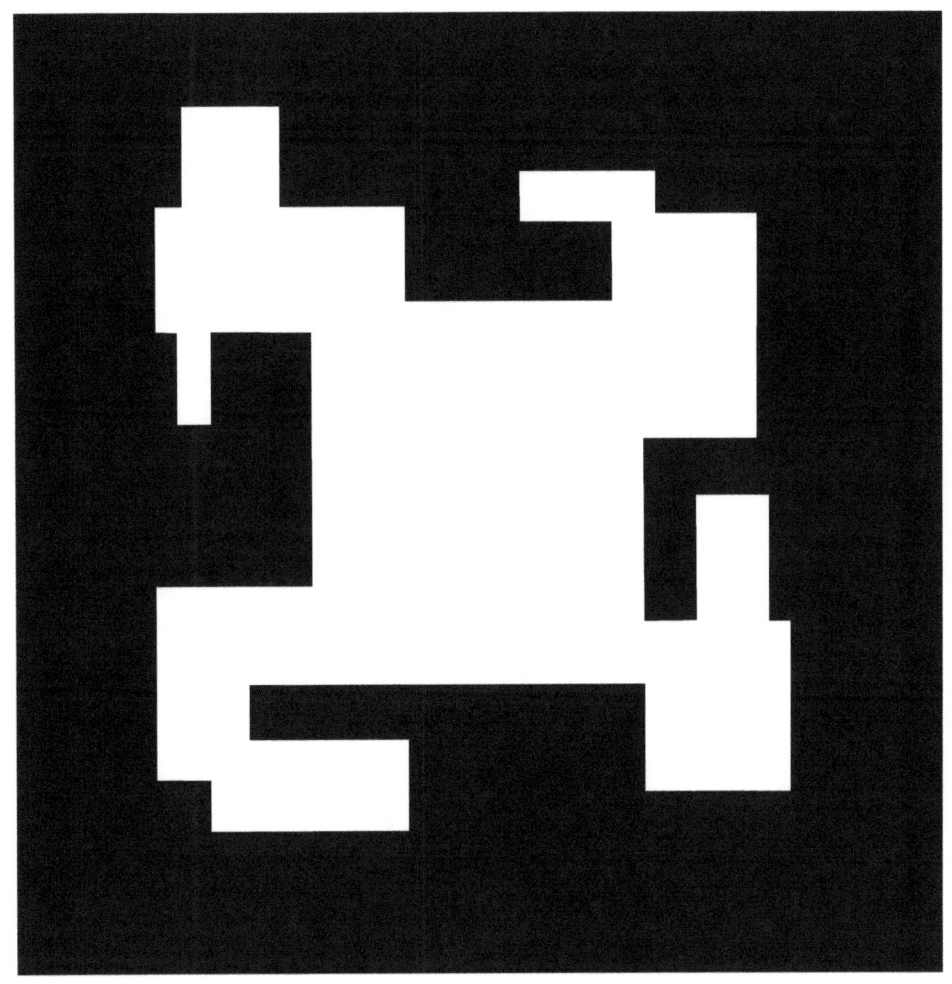

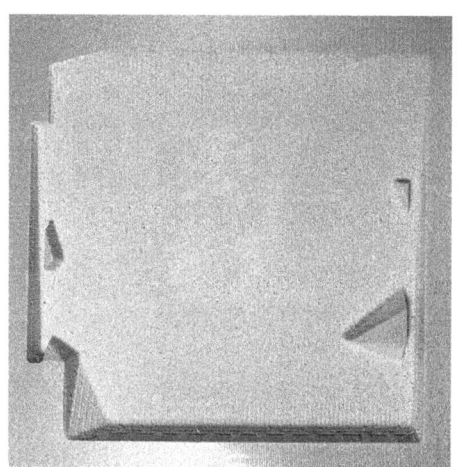

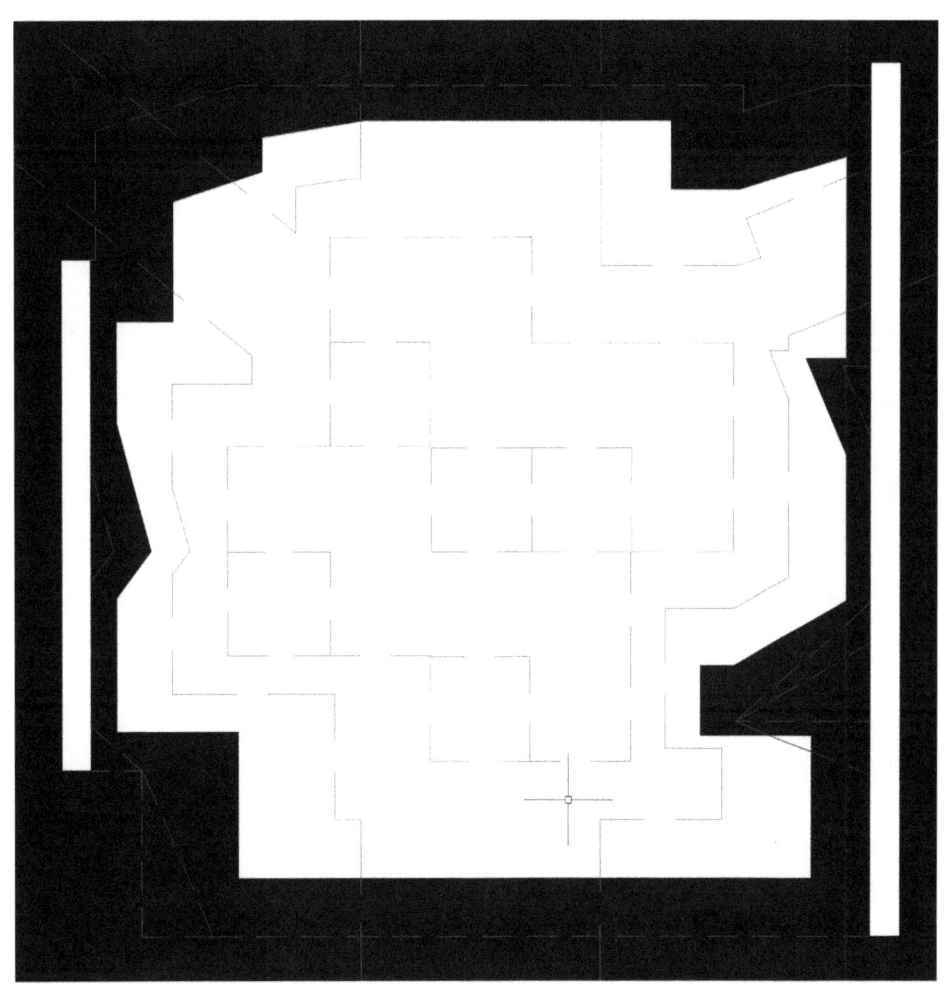

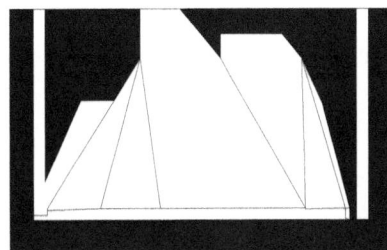
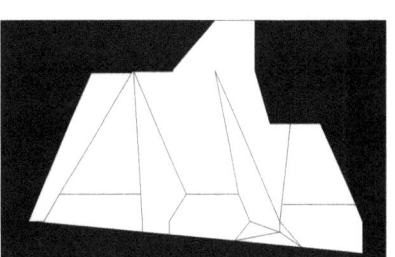

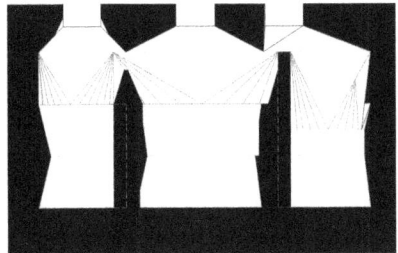 

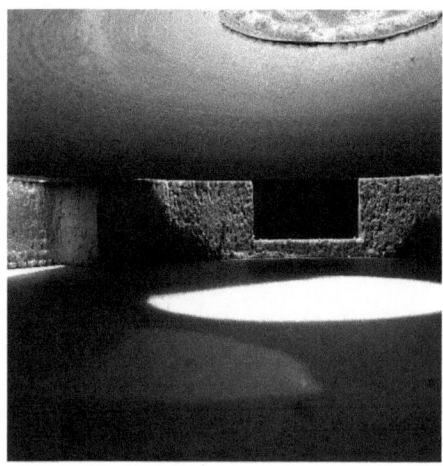
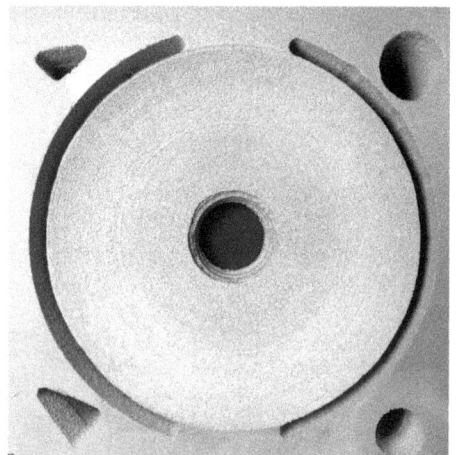

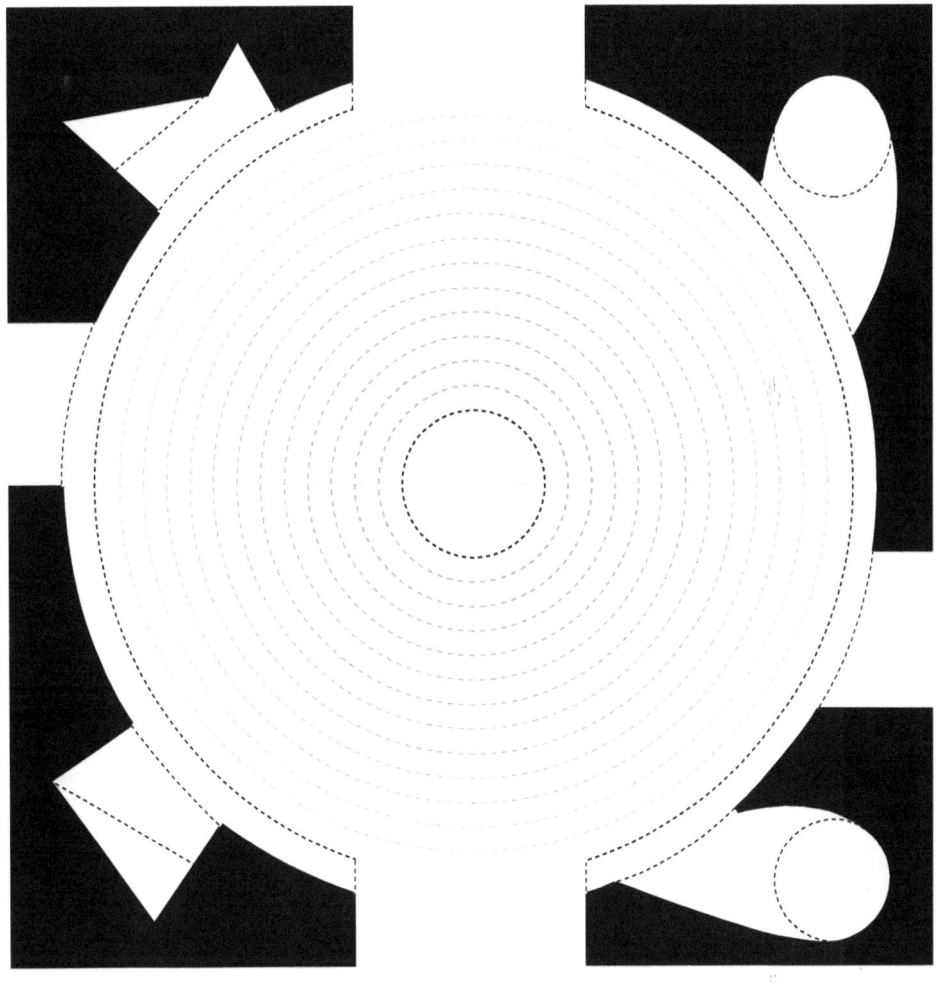

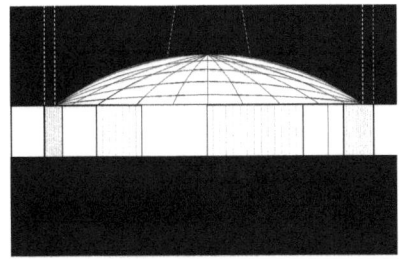
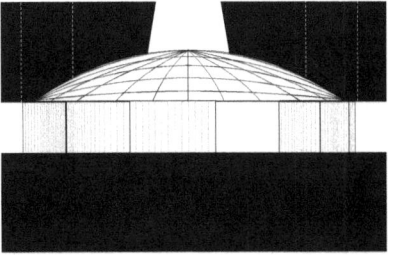

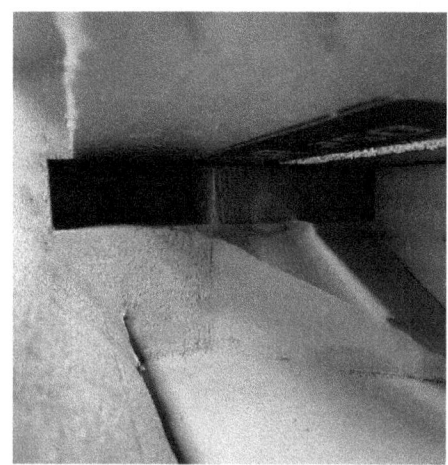

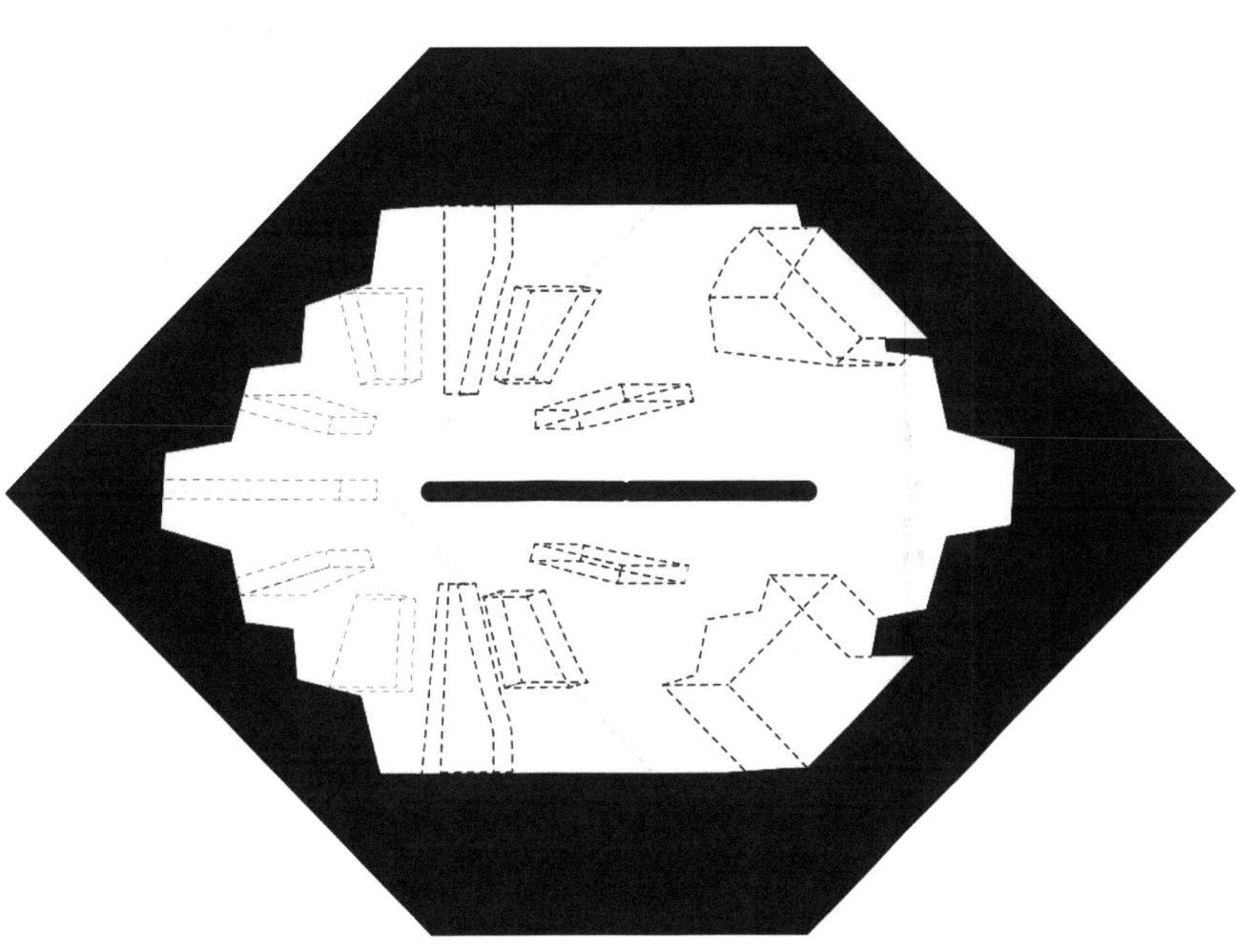

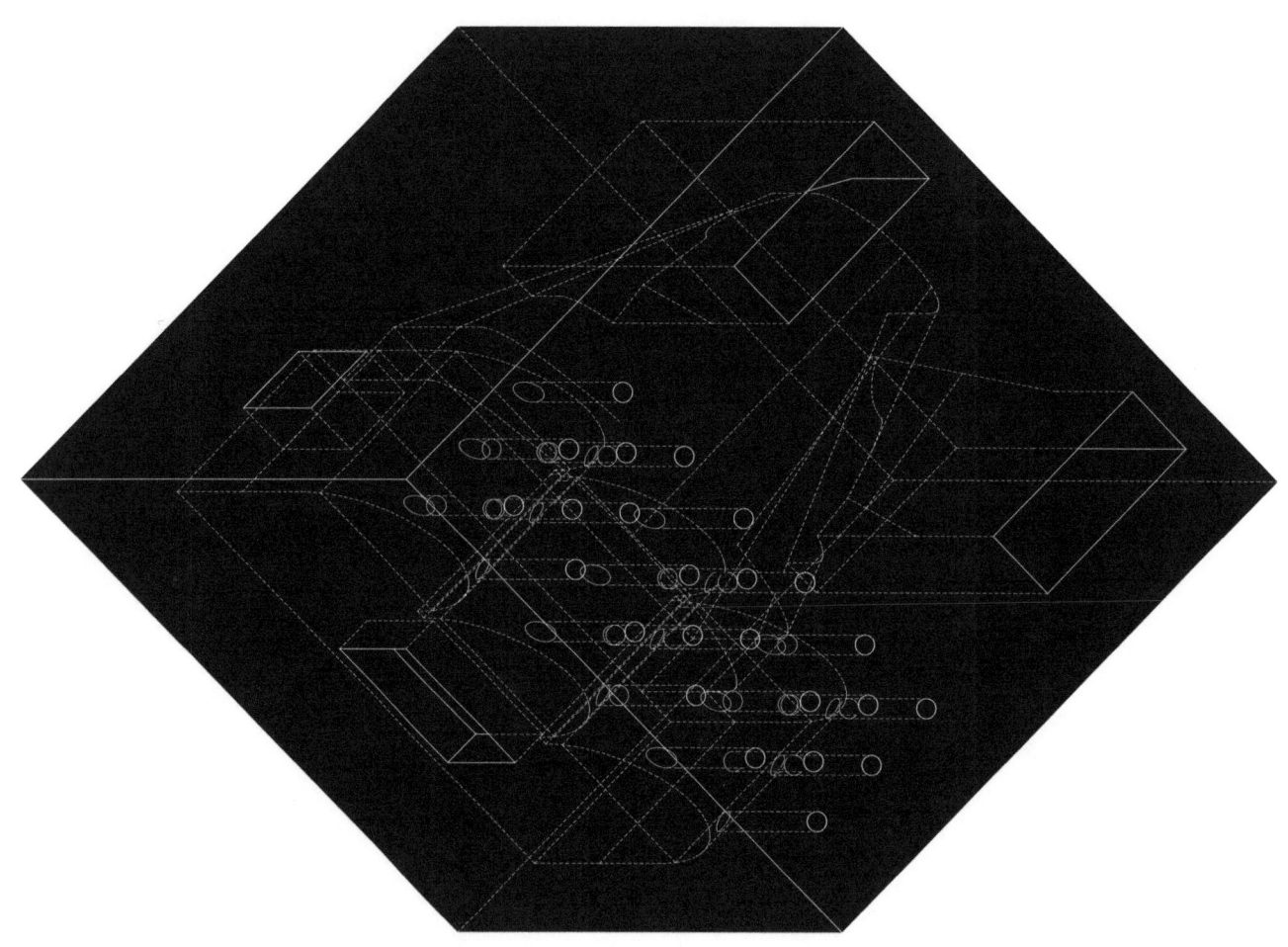

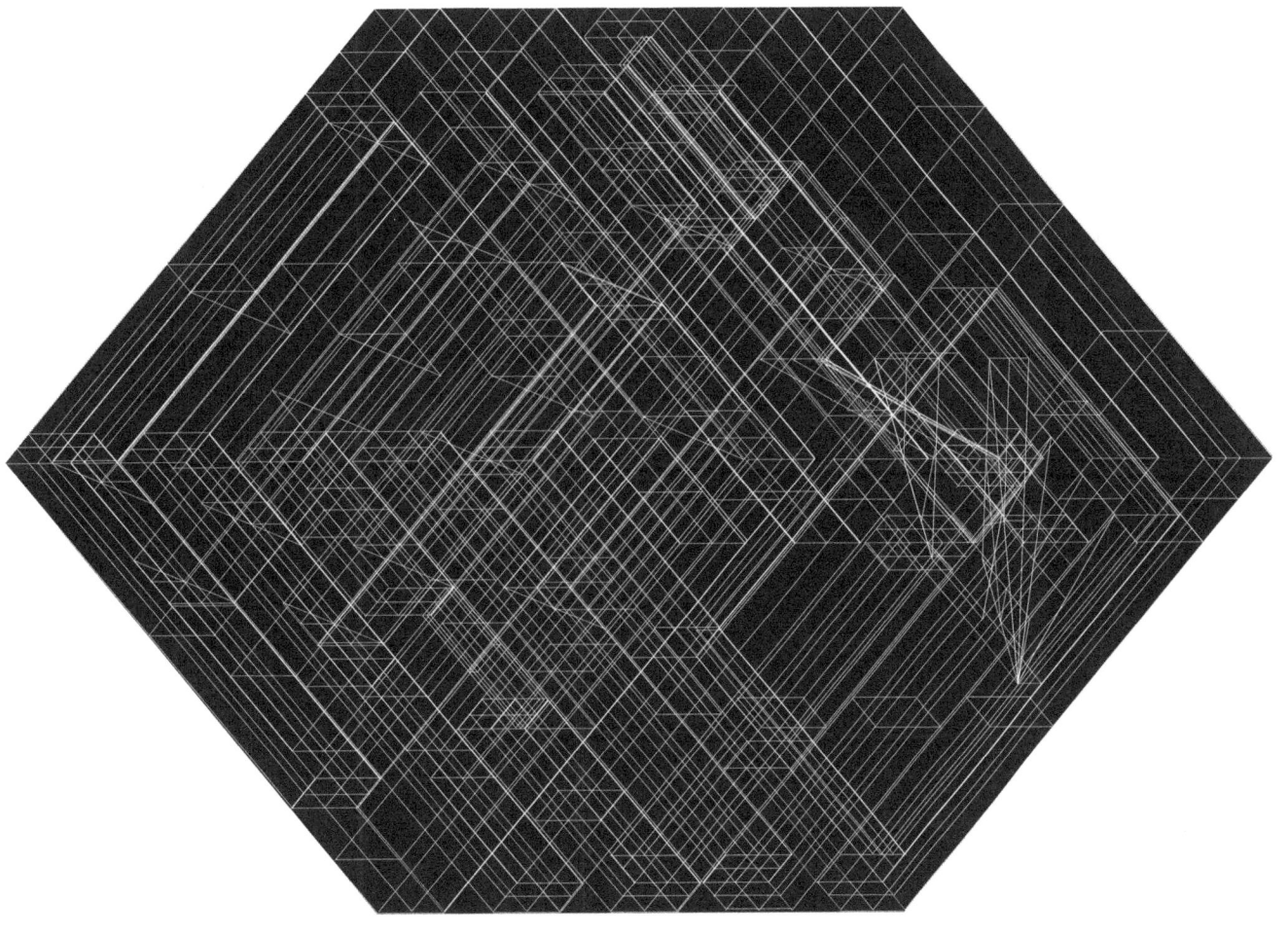

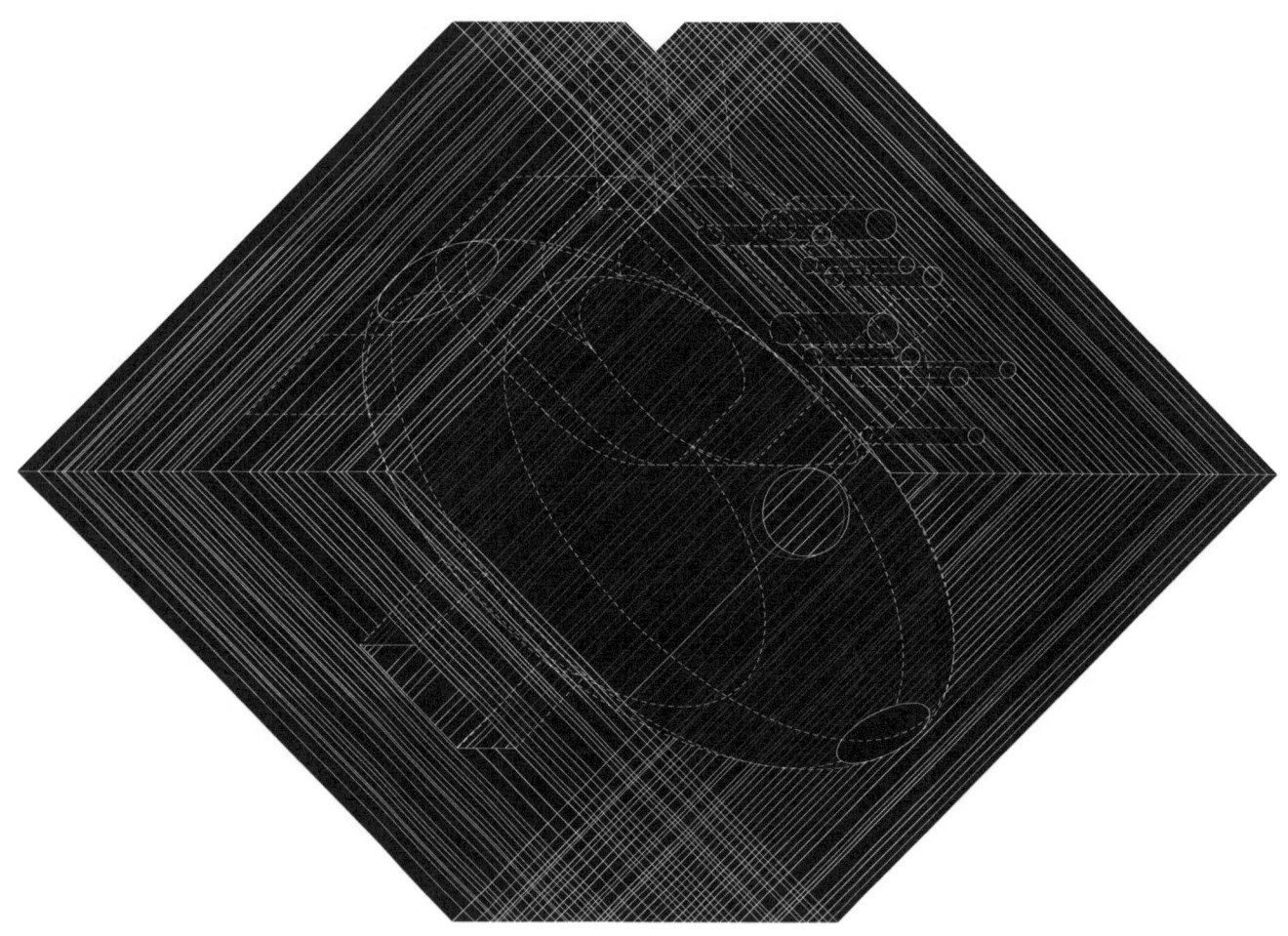

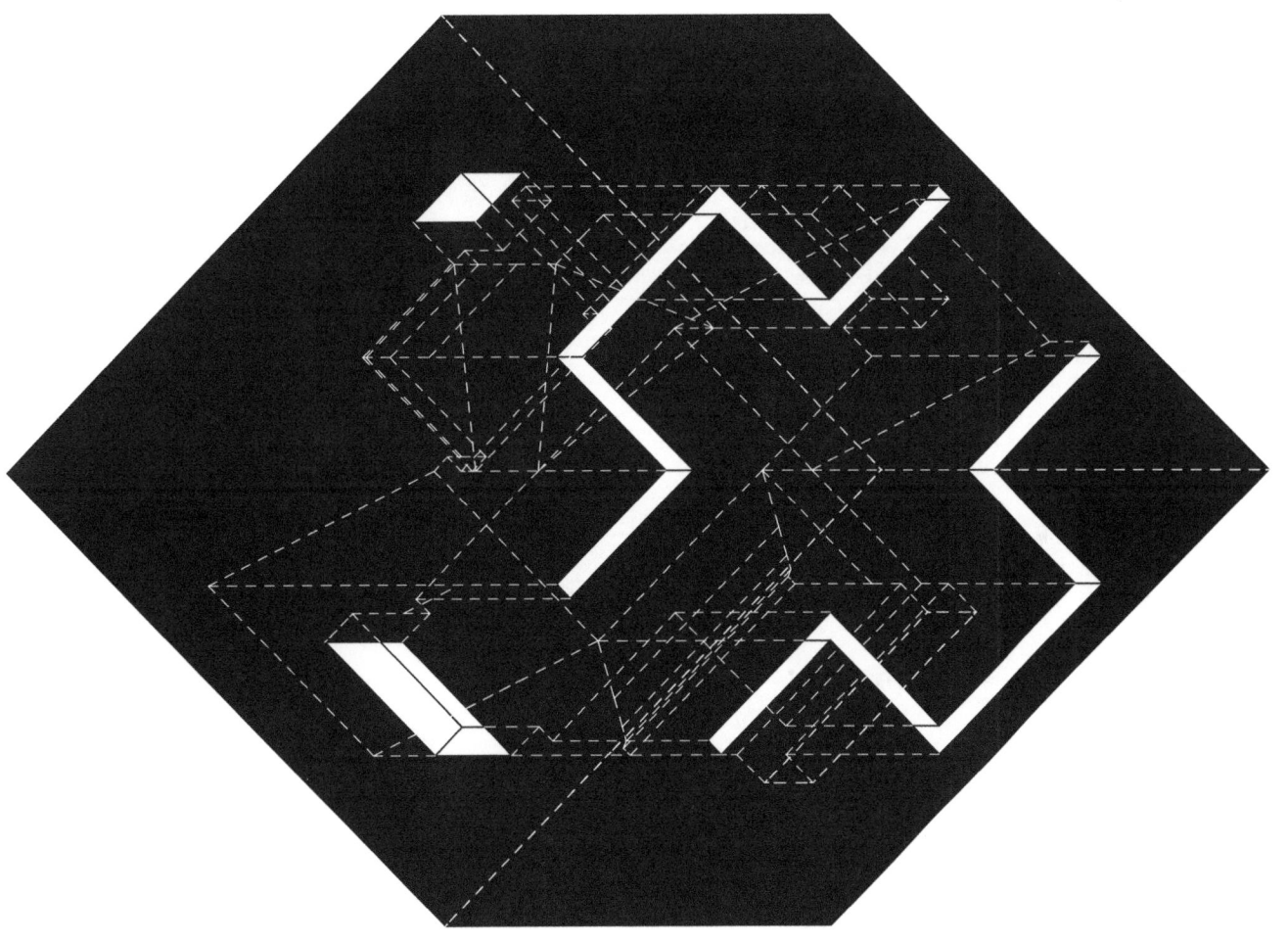

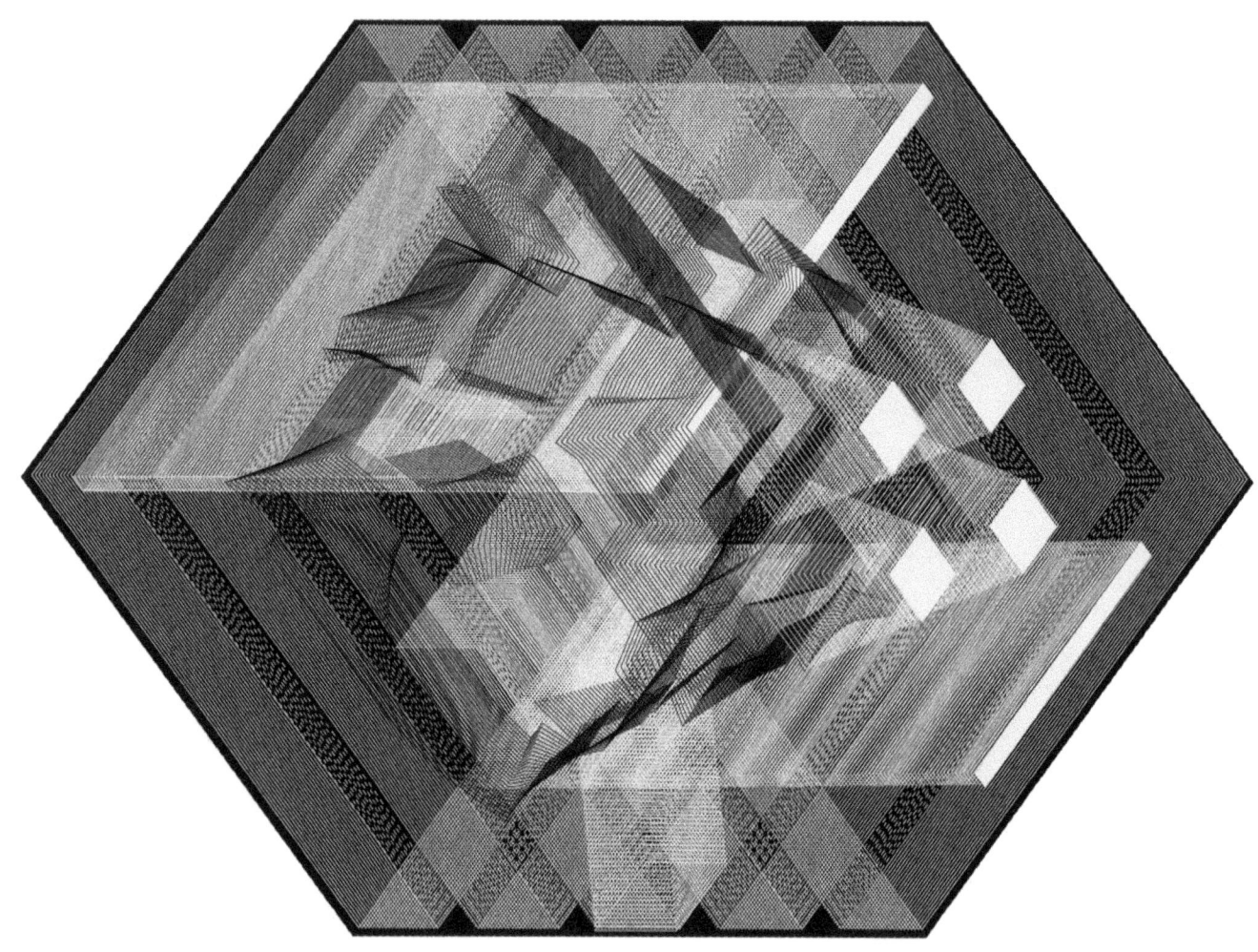

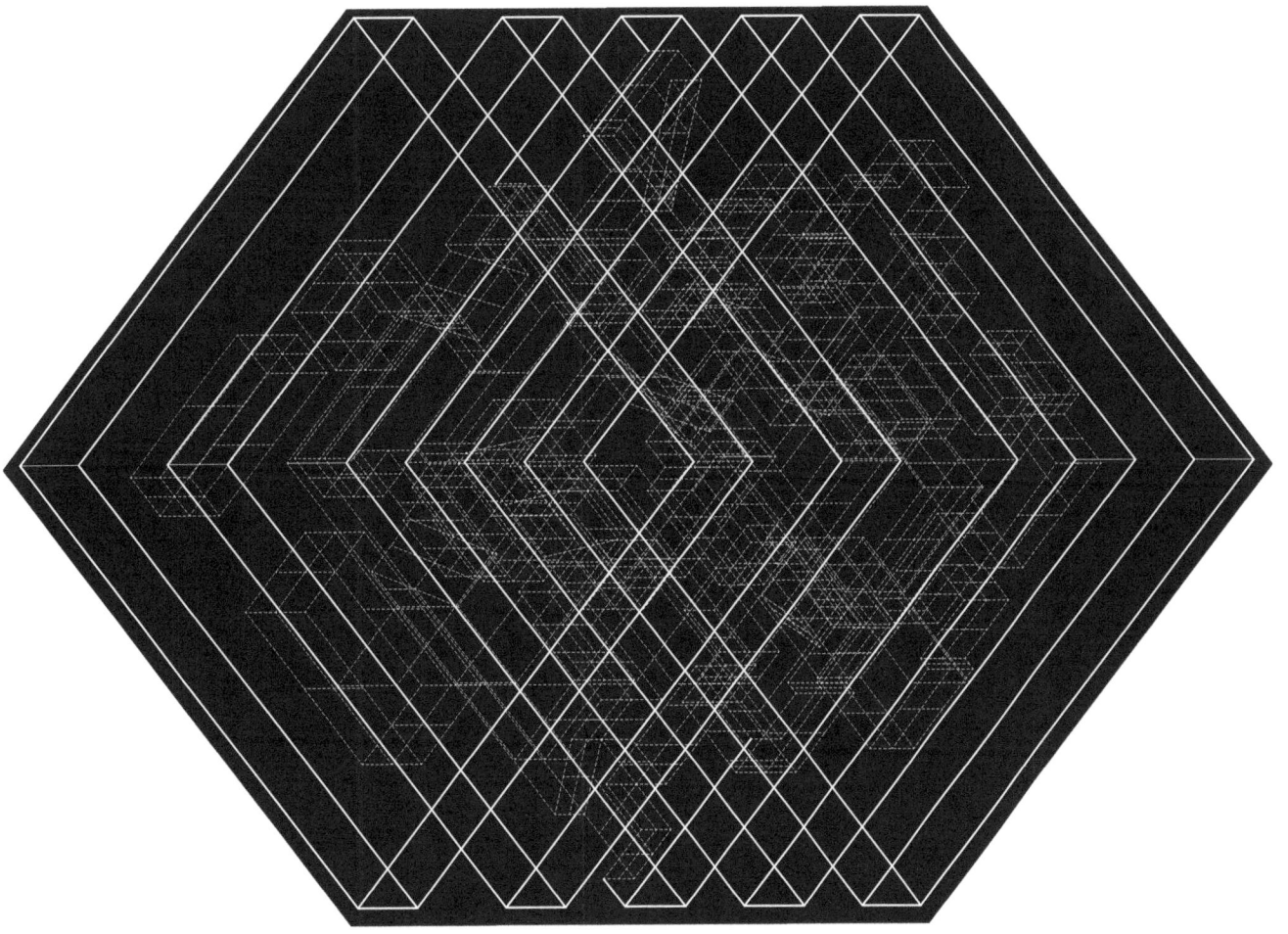

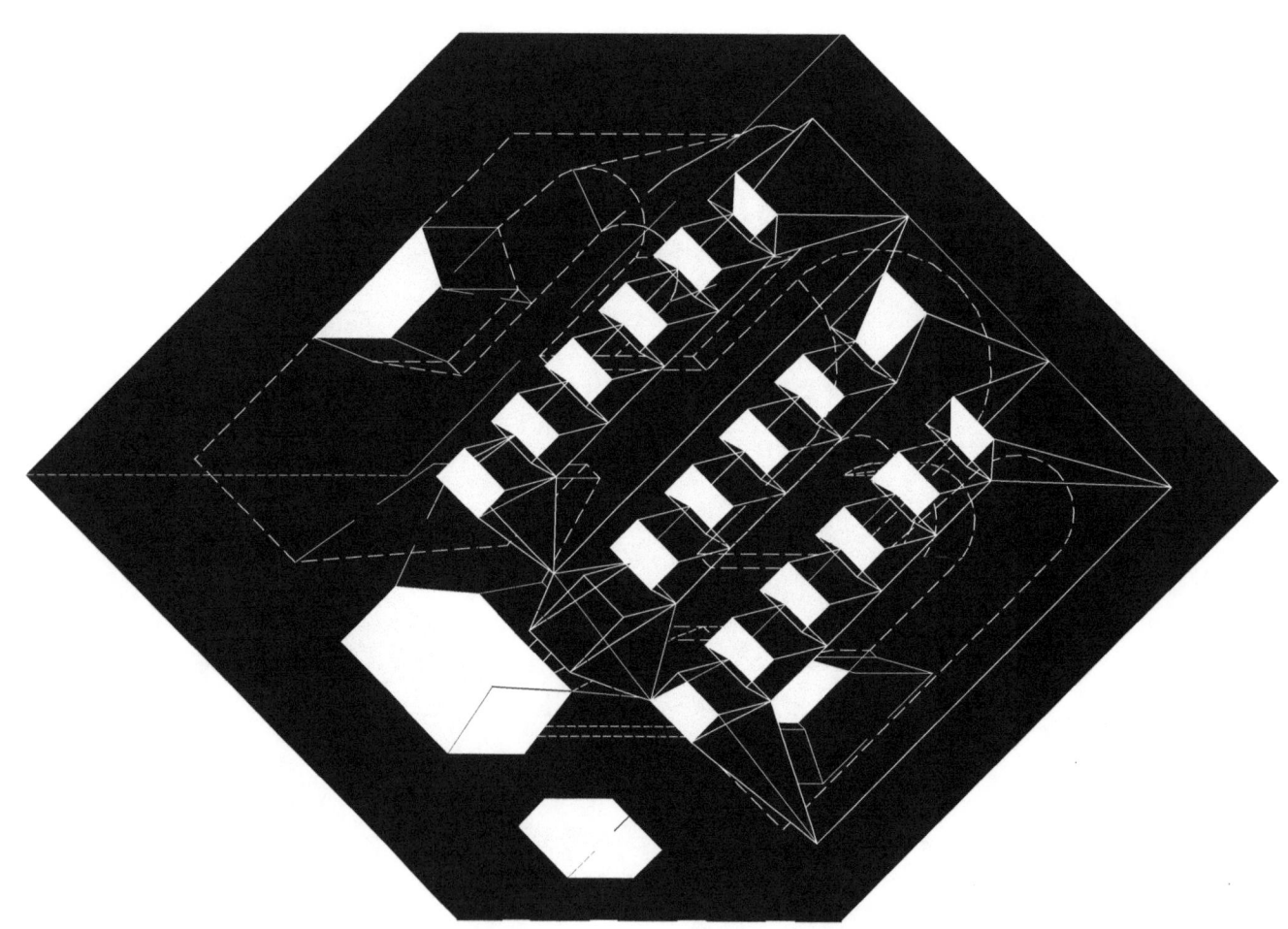

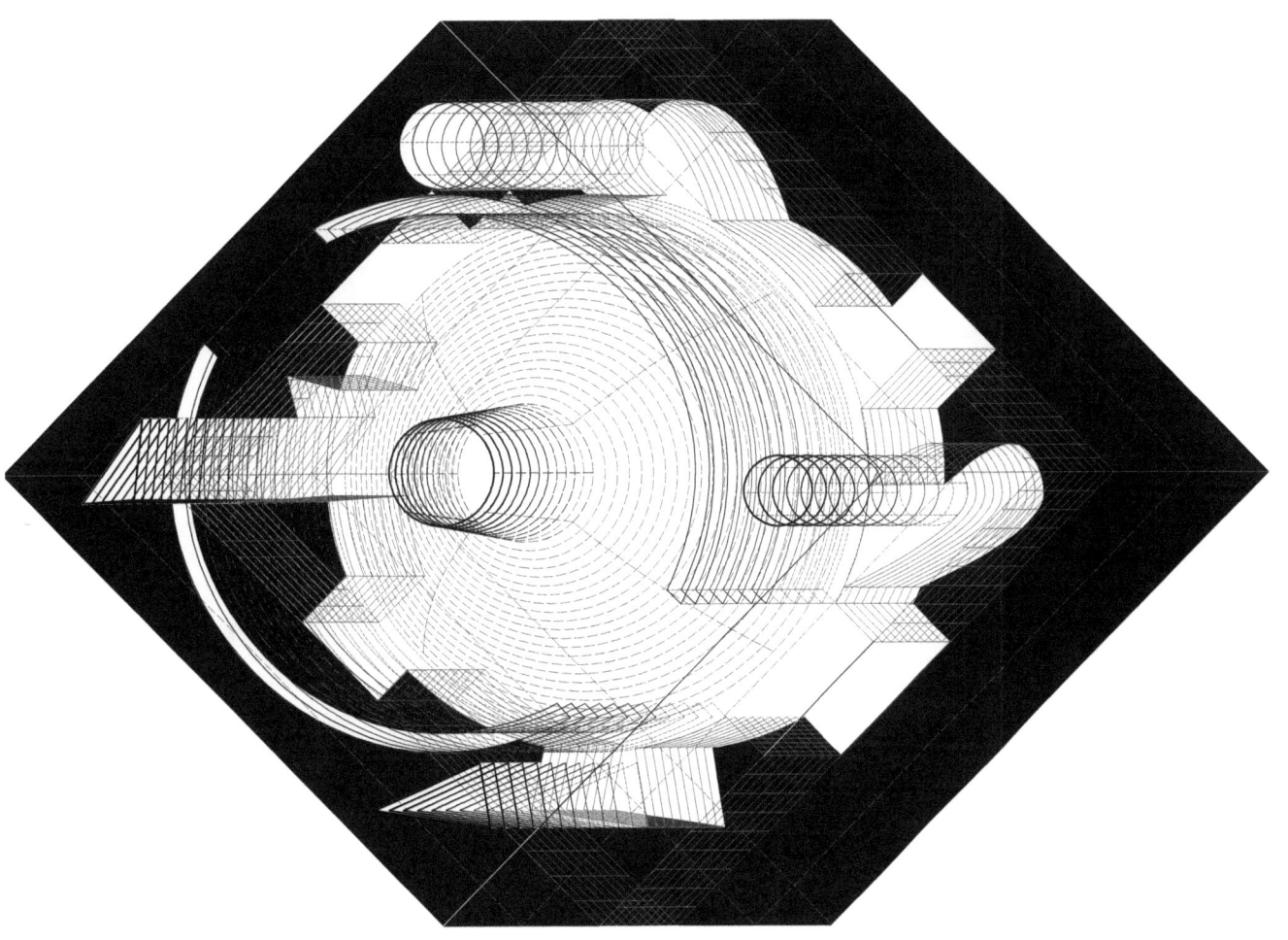

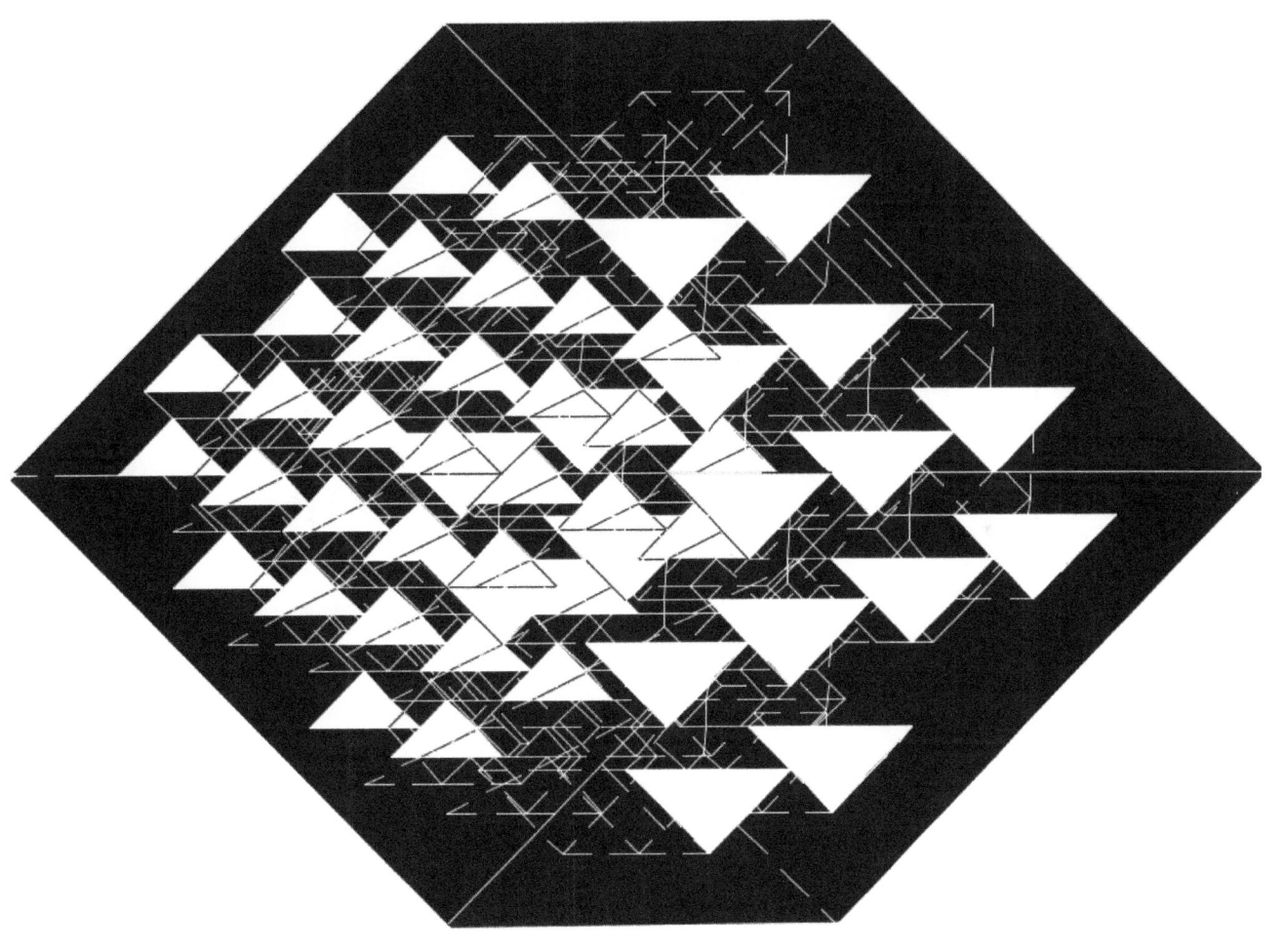

Rock Of Ages Quarry, Barre, VT
Photo by Brooke McDermott (left)

Textures at Rock of Ages
Photos by Lauren Scheid

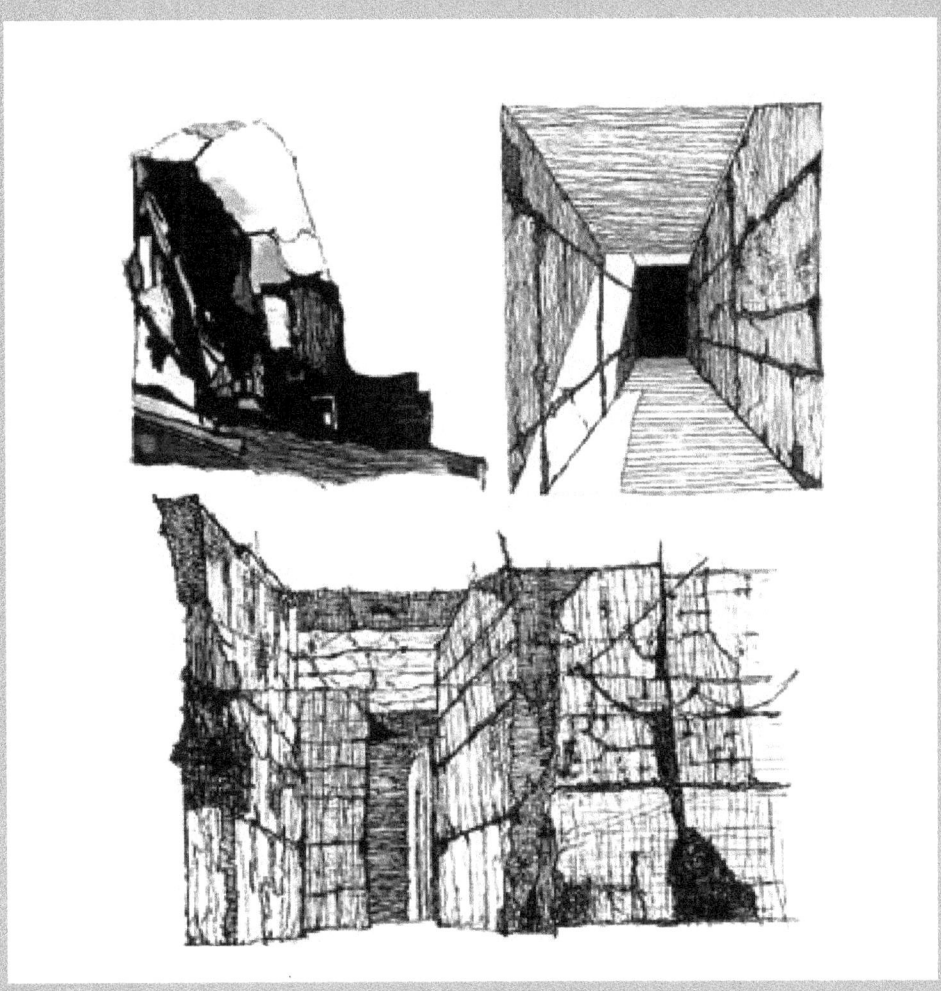

Rock Of Ages Quarry, Barre, VT
Drawings by Mitchell Dasilva

Part Two
A Quarry, A Site, A Memory

George B. Milne, one of the three founders of Rock of Ages, opened his first granite manufacturing company in 1885. During the last decade of the nineteenth century, he had several short-lived partnerships. The company operated quarries in Graniteville, selling Medium Barre and specializing in Dark Barre granite. In 1914, BM&V hired Hayes Advertising of Burlington, Vermont, to increase the visibility of their national advertising campaign. In that same year, the name "Rock of Ages" emerged. By 1924, so many people were coming to see the "holes" that BM&V added a special viewing room in the floor plan of their new machinists' building.

The understanding of a site requires a full and detailed knowledge of its physical and historical conditions.

On that end, the project starts by gathering all relevant information about this specific location in order to form an accurate and comprehensive definition of the site. Once the site is fully comprehended, general strategies are defined, both theoretical and practical, on how to intervene in a site of such special characteristics. The definition of the program is relatively open, although it should include at least the following two parts: an interpretation center and a small retreat hotel.

In addition to the cold tectonics of construction and program solving, the project should respond with the poetics of pure form, twilight, mass and even the immaterial relationships which magically define a place and provide richness beyond pragmatic functionality.

Rock Of Ages Quarry, Barre, VT

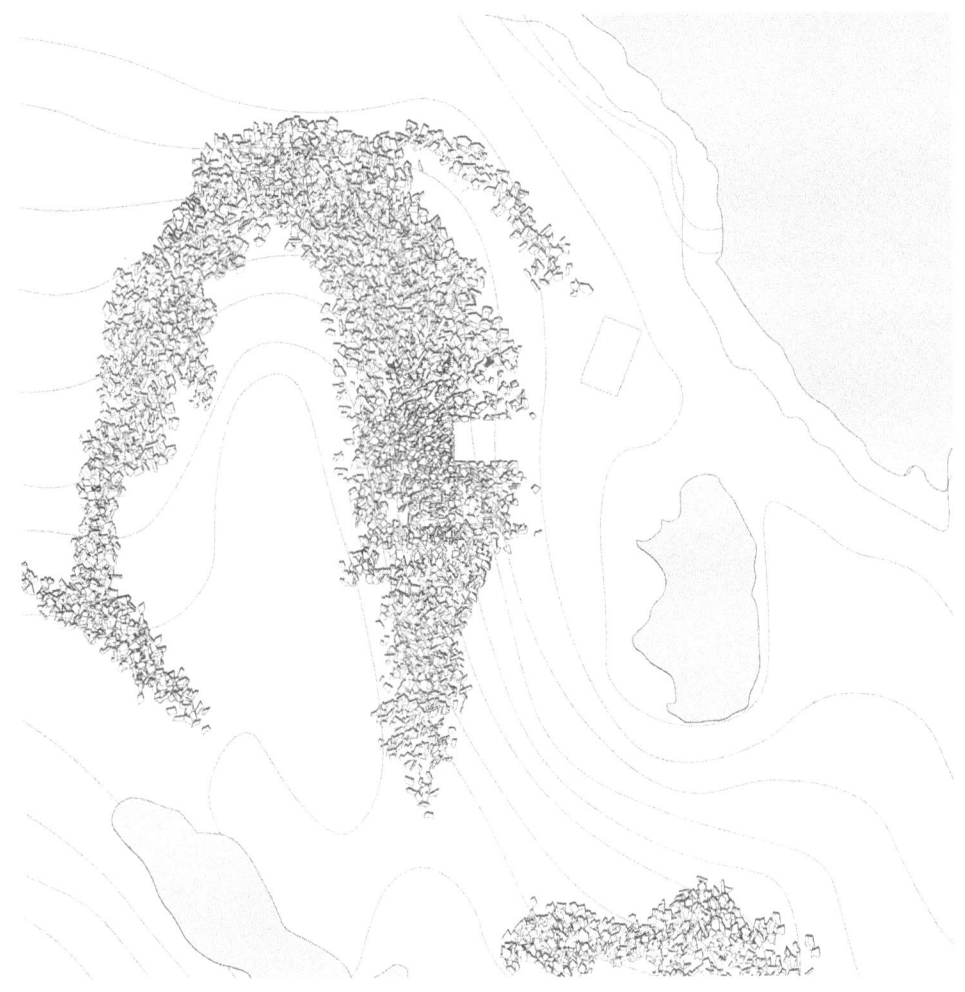

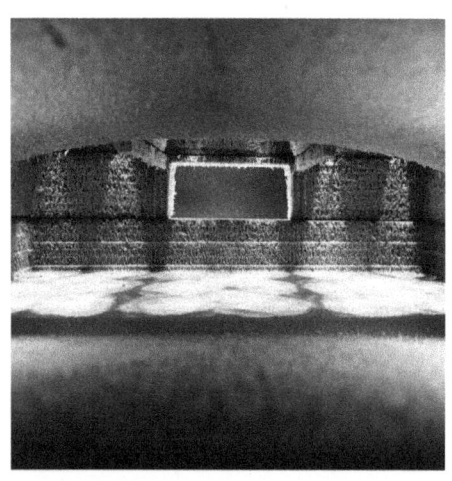

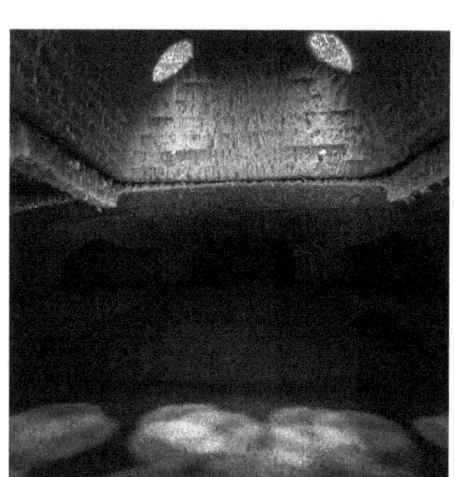

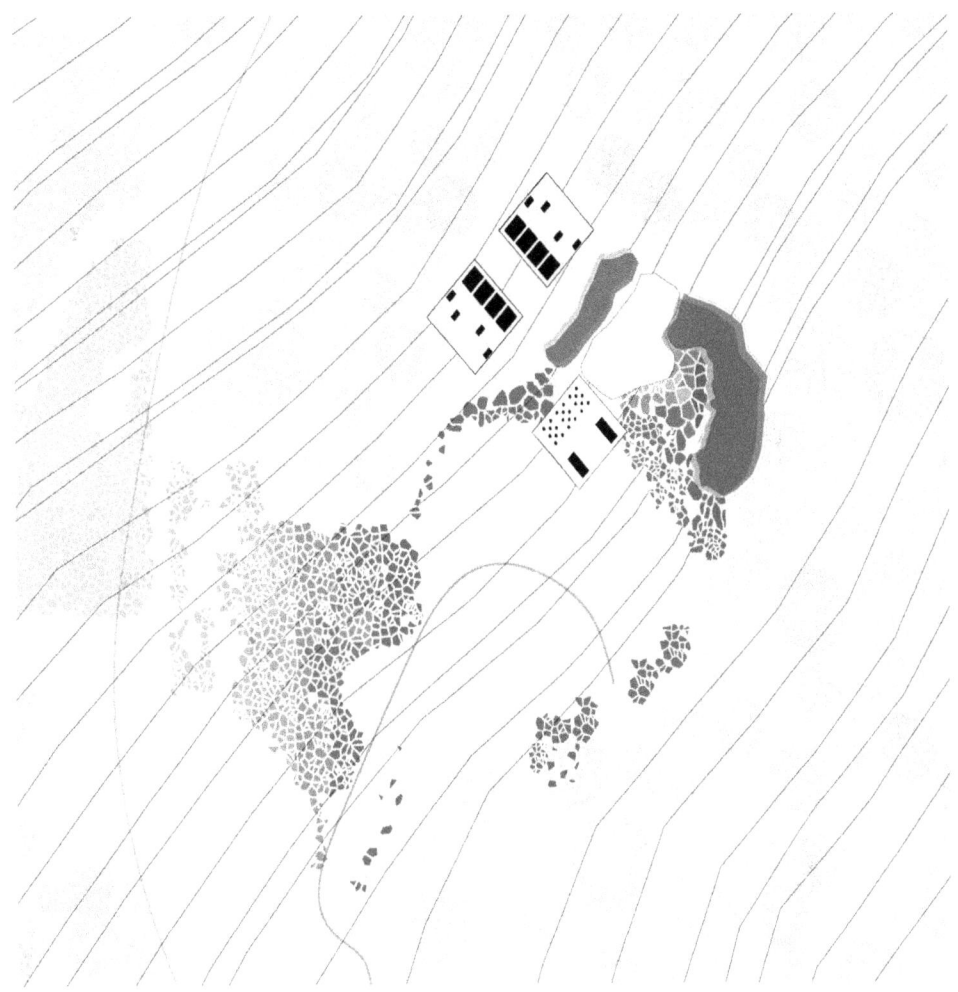

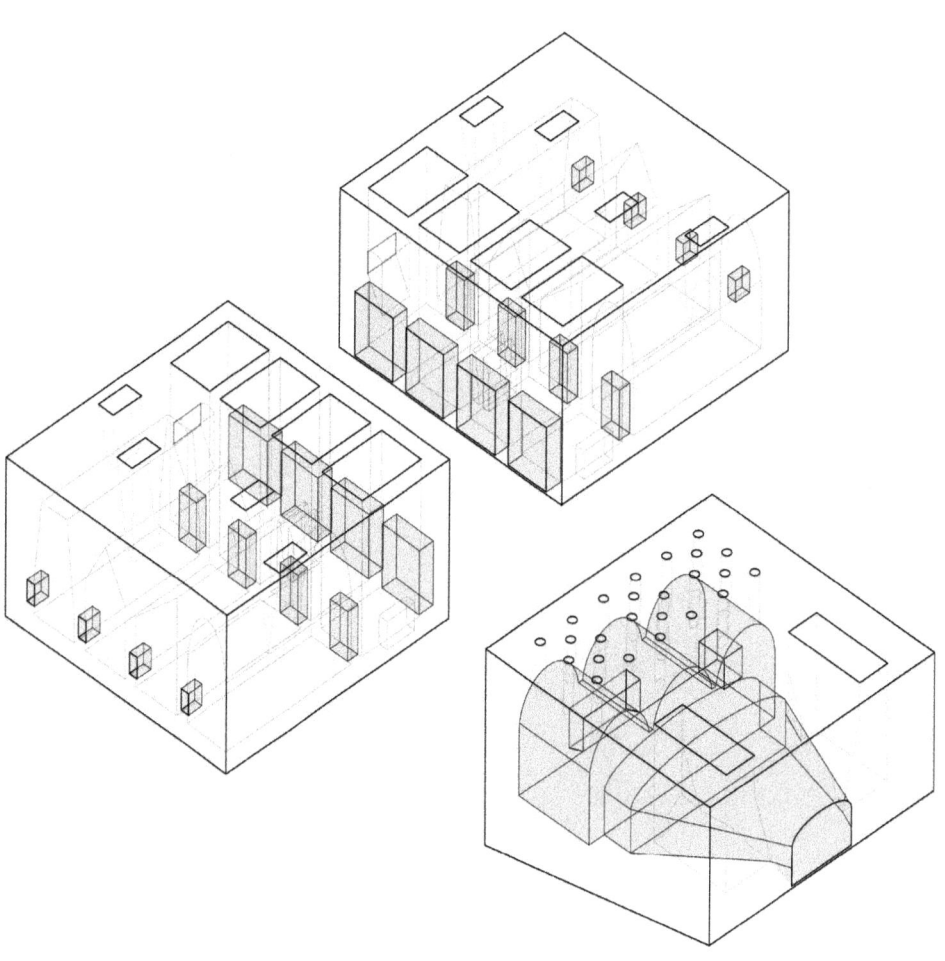

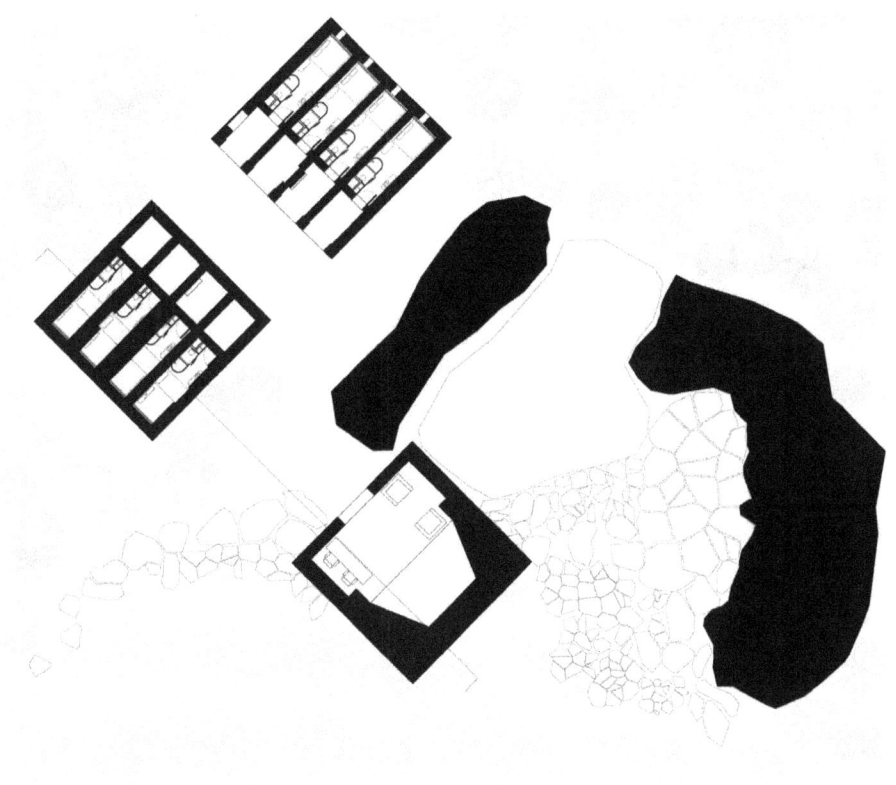

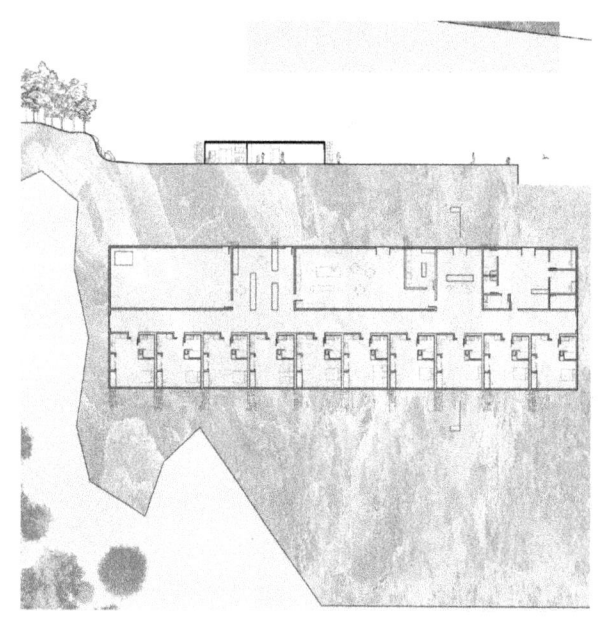

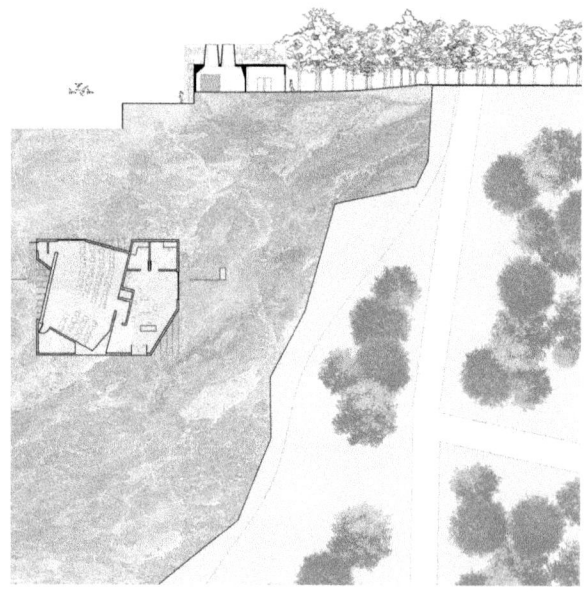

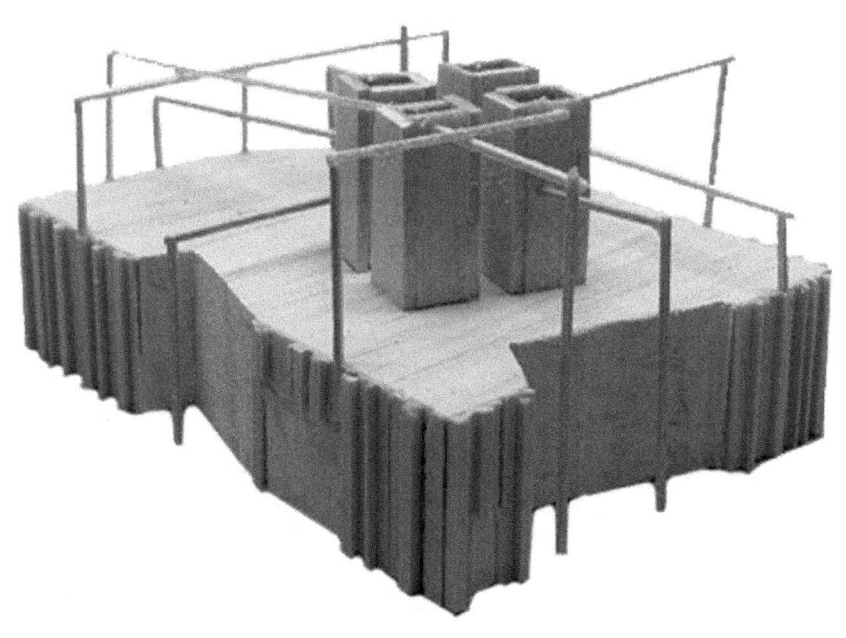

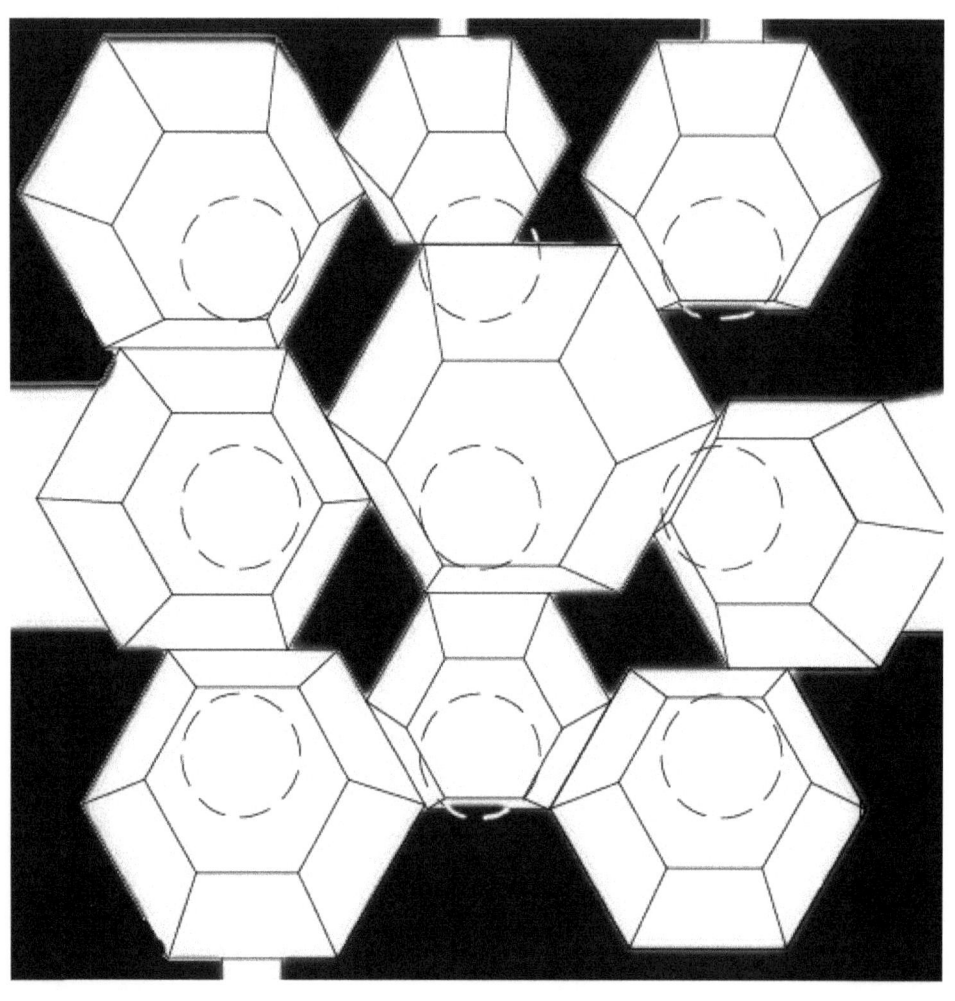

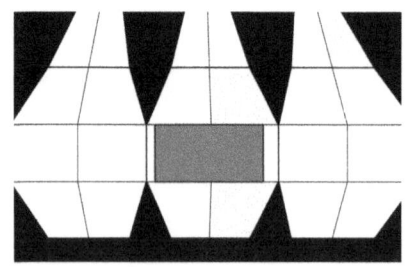
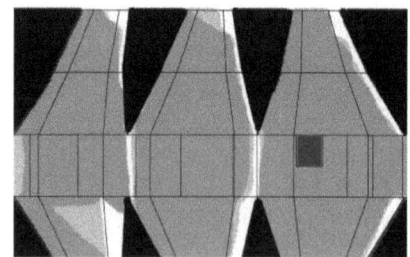

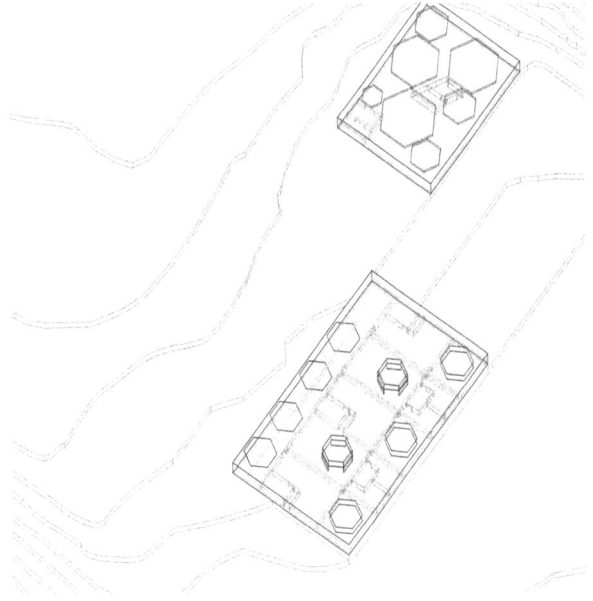

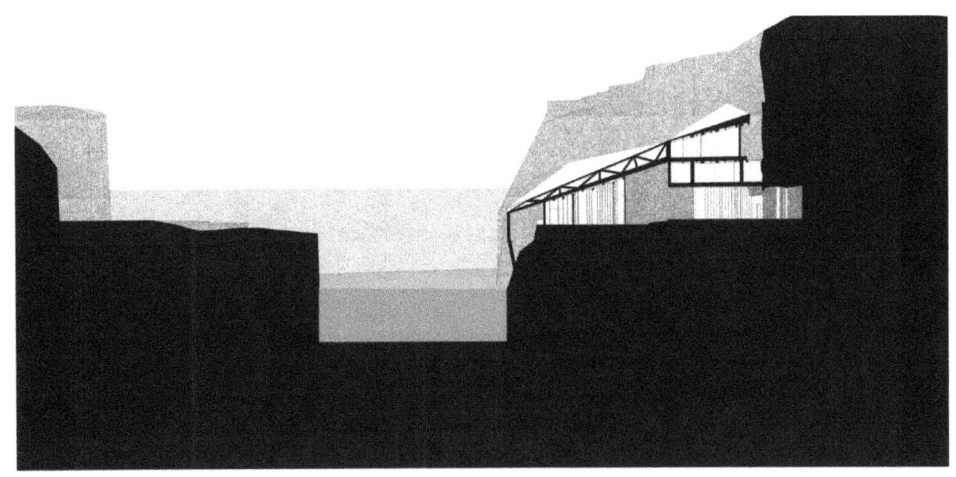

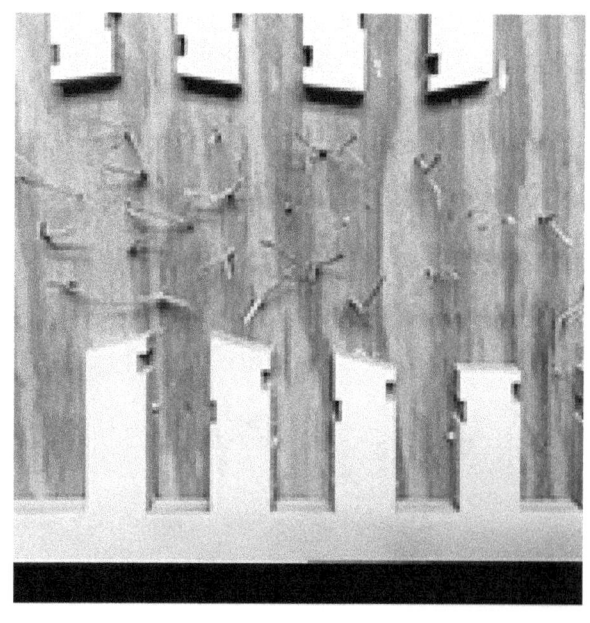

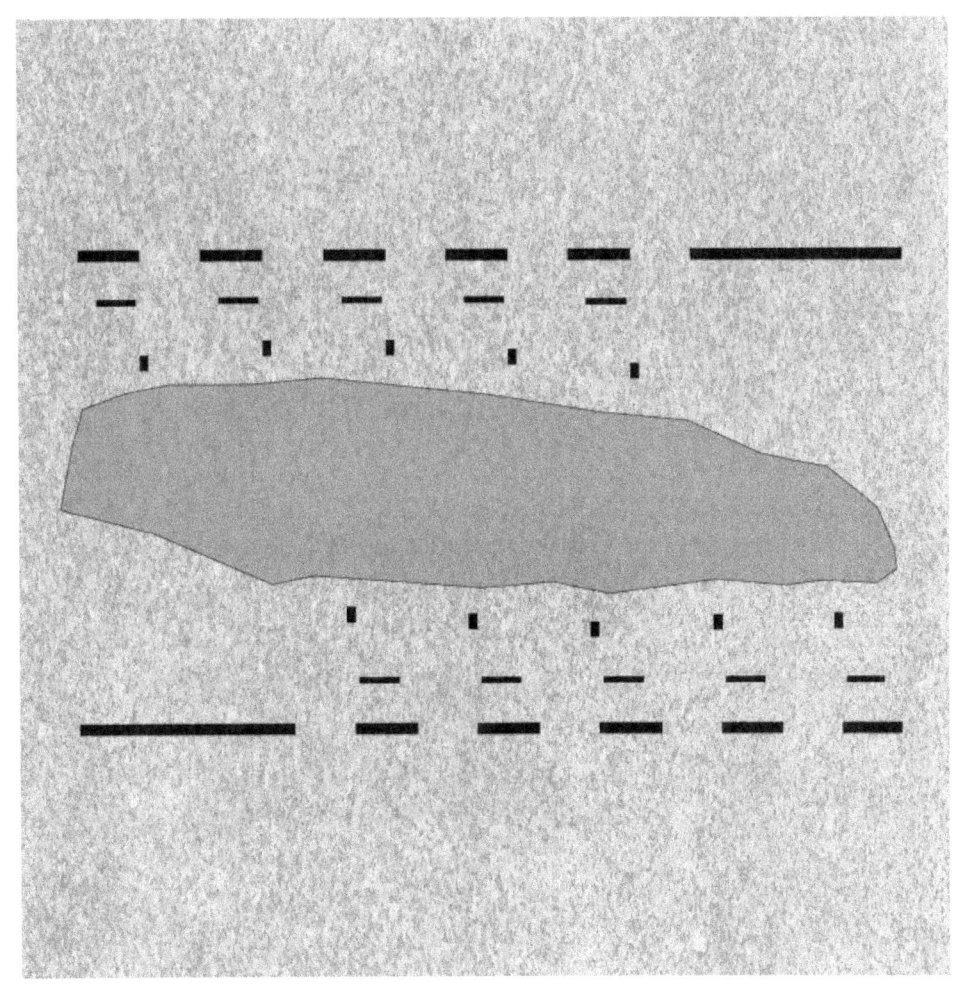

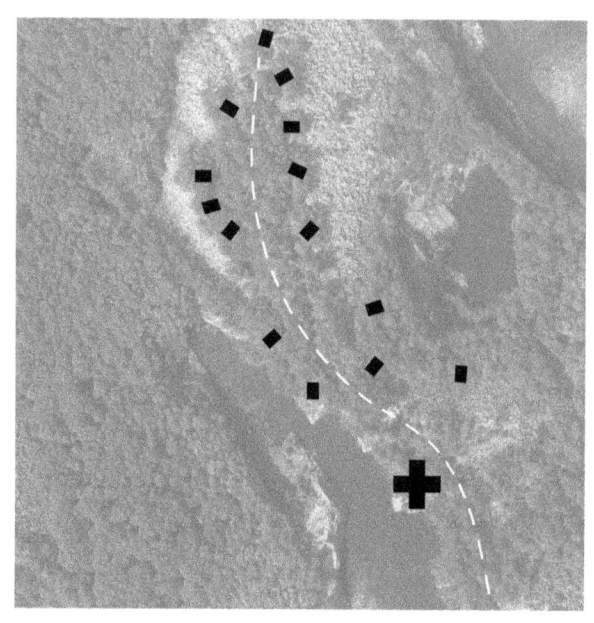

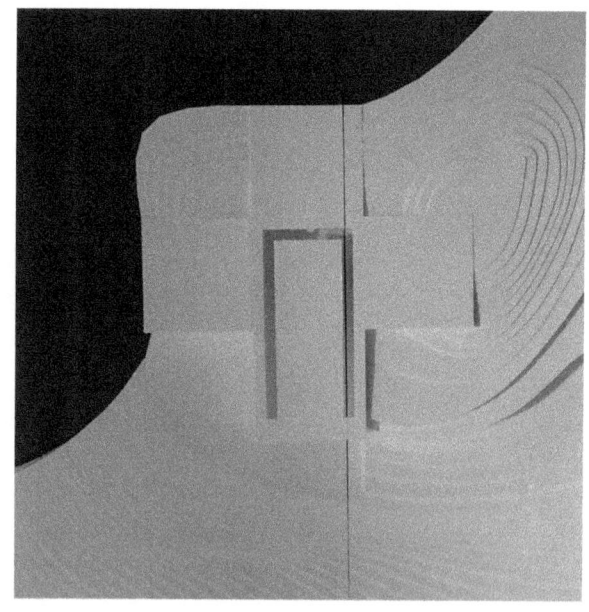

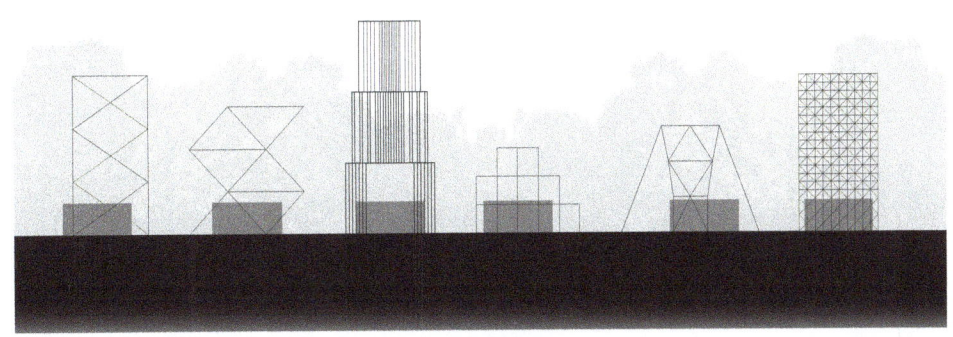

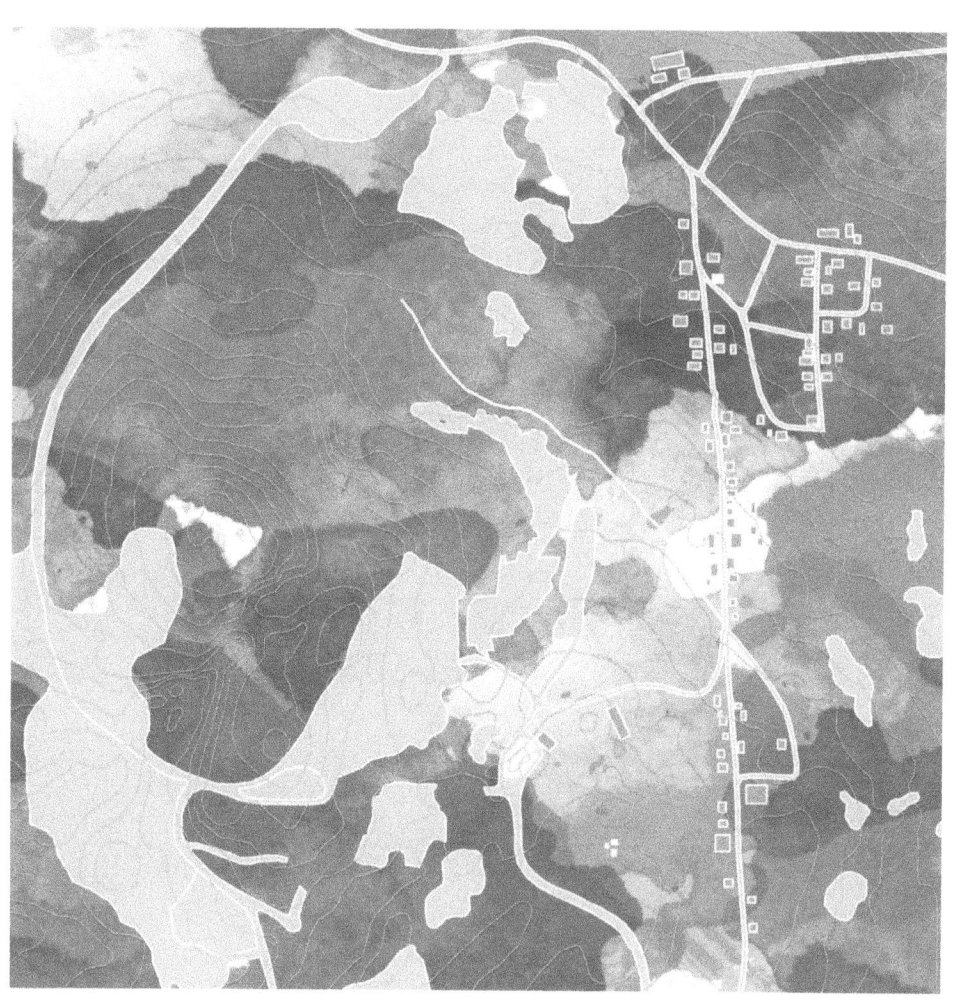

Hypogeans
Space that Matters

Edited by Rubén Alcolea

Files is a platform for sharing ideas, projects and research developed within the academia.

Credits:
Mitchell Dasilva 40, 64-65, 77, 82-83, 110-113
Anakin Geisle 22, 48-49, 69
Brooke McDermott 26, 52-53, 78-79, 86-87
Lauren Ostrzyzek 32, 58-59, 75, 108-109
Jessica Raccio 28, 54-55, 72, 88-92
Mark Reul 38, 100-101
Robert Rice 42
Lisett Ronchi 36, 62-63, 76, 102-103
Adam Royle 20, 46-47, 68, 98-99
Lauren Scheid 34, 60-61, 74, 96-97
Kyle Sheehan 30, 56-57, 73, 106-107
Brianna Valcourt 24, 50-51, 70, 92-95
Robert Ward 46, 66-67, 71, 104-105

www.ingramcontent.com/pod-product-compliance
Lightning Source LLC
Chambersburg PA
CBHW041157120626
46547CB00020B/3249